*The beginning of anxiety is the end of faith,
and the beginning of true faith is the end of anxiety.*

—George Müller

# Love's a Mystery

Love's a Mystery in Sleepy Hollow, New York
Love's a Mystery in Cape Disappointment, Washington
Love's a Mystery in Cut and Shoot, Texas
Love's a Mystery in Nameless, Tennessee
Love's a Mystery in Hazardville, Connecticut
Love's a Mystery in Deadwood, Oregon
Love's a Mystery in Gnaw Bone, Indiana
Love's a Mystery in Tombstone, Arizona
Love's a Mystery in Peculiar, Missouri
Love's a Mystery in Crooksville, Ohio
Love's a Mystery in Last Chance, Iowa
Love's a Mystery in Panic, Pennsylvania

Love's a Mystery

*in*

# Panic PA

# Elizabeth Ludwig & Barbara Early

Love's a Mystery is a trademark of Guideposts.

Published by Guideposts Books & Inspirational Media
100 Reserve Road, Suite E200
Danbury, CT 06810
Guideposts.org

Copyright © 2023 by Guideposts. All rights reserved.

This book, or parts thereof, may not be reproduced, stored in a retrieval system, or transmitted in any form or by any means, electronic, mechanical, photocopying, recording, or otherwise, without the written permission of the publisher.

This is a work of fiction. While the settings of Love's a Mystery as presented in this series is fictional, the locations actually exist, and some places and characters may be based on actual places and people whose identities have been used with permission or fictionalized to protect their privacy. Apart from the actual people, events, and locales that figure into the fiction narrative, all other names, characters, businesses, and events are the creation of the author's imagination, and any resemblance to actual persons or events is coincidental.

Every attempt has been made to credit the sources of copyrighted material used in this book. If any such acknowledgment has been inadvertently omitted or miscredited, receipt of such information would be appreciated.

Scripture references are from the following sources: *The Holy Bible, King James Version* (KJV). *The Holy Bible, New International Version* (NIV). Copyright ©1973, 1978, 1984, 2011 by Biblica, Inc. Used by permission of Zondervan. All rights reserved worldwide. www.zondervan.com

Cover and interior design by Müllerhaus
Cover illustration by Dan Burr at Illustration Online LLC.
Typeset by Aptara, Inc.

ISBN 978-1-959634-14-0 (hardcover)
ISBN 978-1-959634-18-8 (epub)
ISBN 978-1-959634-16-4 (epdf)

Printed and bound in the United States of America
10 9 8 7 6 5 4 3 2 1

# A Heart Divided

by
Elizabeth Ludwig

*There is no fear in love; but perfect love casteth out fear: because fear hath torment. He that feareth is not made perfect in love.*

—1 John 4:18 (kjv)

# Chapter One

*Panic, Pennsylvania*
*July 1917*

"There he is…that *Mueller* boy."

The derisive words rasped like sandpaper on Hannah Walker's skin, as irritating and abrasive as the murmurings of treason and spies that poisoned every corner of their small town. Daily, Hannah told herself she would have no part of them. In fact, if she had any sense, she'd ignore the whispers and march right out of Smith's General Store…but she didn't, because with curiosity prickling the nape of her neck, she couldn't help but look.

A few feet away, Niklas Mueller browsed an assortment of pots and pans hanging from hooks in the window. Outlined against the hot July sun streaming through the glass, his shoulders looked even broader, the tilt of his head prouder than when she'd last seen him.

Lifting his hand, Niklas snagged one of the pots and then turned. Hair dark as pitch feathered out from beneath the brim of a battered brown hat. Eyes and eyebrows to match filled a face bronzed by the sun.

For a second, their eyes met. Held. Slowing time. Until a breathless whisper at Hannah's elbow broke her trance.

"Did you hear that? I *told* you people didn't trust the Muellers."

Sucking in a breath, Hannah dragged her gaze away to scowl at her friend. "Edith Davis, you've known Niklas your whole life. You know the rumors about him and his father are nothing more than gossip spurred by the war. And if you haven't noticed, he's hardly a *boy*."

Edith's eyebrows rose an inch to meet the flowers dripping from her linen cloche hat. "Does that mean you *have* noticed?"

Hannah pursed her lips and reached around Edith for a bolt of plain cotton fabric. "I was merely making an observation."

"As was I," Edith whispered. Then she drew up short and straightened, her brown eyes widening. "Oh."

"Good afternoon, Miss Davis."

Hannah immediately recognized the voice rumbling over her shoulder. She blew out a breath and turned.

Niklas touched his finger to the brim of his hat, his sooty brown gaze coming to rest on her. "Miss Walker."

Hearing her surname on his lips was quite different than when they were growing up and attending the schoolhouse at the edge of town. Then, they'd thought nothing of calling each other by their Christian names. Now, hearing him sound so formal left her feeling a bit flustered.

She inclined her head and reciprocated in kind. "Mr. Mueller."

A smile twitched his lips, as though he alone were privy to her secret thoughts. But of course, that couldn't be. She ignored the urge to press her fingers to her warm cheeks and instead motioned to the pot in his hand. "I didn't realize you cook."

Niklas's grin grew. "It's only Papa and me, so I suppose one of us has to. Either that or starve."

"Yes, well, true enough, I suppose." A second heat wave burned across Hannah's skin.

Niklas nodded to the fabric clutched in her arms. "I didn't realize you could sew."

She couldn't. She despised the chore and complained about it regularly, which explained the grin that was even now widening his full lips. Depositing the bolt of fabric back on the table, Hannah shook her head and smoothed her hands over the folds of her blue skirt. "Edith and I were just browsing."

The mention of Edith's name was like a bucket of water dousing Niklas's smile. "Right. Forgive me for interrupting." He pulled back a step and hitched his thumb toward the register. "I should go. Papa will be waiting."

"Of course. Please tell Mr. Mueller hello for us." At her side, Edith remained silent, so Hannah prompted her with a sharp nudge of her elbow.

"Ow…um…yes, please." Rubbing her ribs, Edith speared Hannah with a dark glare.

"I will tell him. Good day." Giving a nod to each, Niklas spun and wound past rows of barrels brimming with food goods toward the counter.

"Hannah, why did you say that?" Edith punctuated the question with a stomp of her foot. "Now people will think we like the Muellers."

"We do like the Muellers," Hannah said, loud enough for a couple of curious onlookers lingering nearby to hear. "They have always been good and faithful neighbors, and I challenge anyone to say otherwise."

Both eavesdropping women sniffed at her words and continued meandering down the aisle, away from them.

With them gone, Hannah rounded on Edith. "You've been listening to that Sally Bradshaw again, haven't you? We can't let what she or any other gossips say influence how we feel about the Muellers."

"Why not? They're German, and we *are* at war with Germany." Edith narrowed her eyes and pressed her lips tight.

Hannah inhaled sharply through her nose. "Have you forgotten how Karl Mueller helped your father the day his ox landed in the ditch? What do you think would have happened if it hadn't been for Mr. Mueller and his team of horses?"

Edith's gaze fell. "No, I haven't forgotten."

Hannah leaned closer. "And what about when Mr. Mueller loaded his wagon with vegetables for the Sampsons after those wild boars rooted through their garden? Or when Niklas helped the Van Pelts rebuild their barn after it burned down? Those aren't the only instances, surely. There are plenty of people who can attest to all that the Muellers have done for our community."

Edith's face flushed bright red. "You're…you're right. I shouldn't have said anything. I'm sorry."

Hannah relaxed a bit, but the knot in the pit of her stomach remained. The country had only been at war for a short while. What would happen if it dragged on for months—or years—the way her father feared? What would people like Sally Bradshaw say about the Muellers then? Suddenly, she no longer felt like shopping.

Hannah motioned to the elderly proprietor hovering like a gaunt scarecrow behind the counter. "Likely Mr. Smith has my order ready by now. I should get home."

"Me too." Edith grasped her arm. "Oh, but Hannah, you never said if you're planning on going to the church picnic." Her eyes brightened. "All our friends will be there."

Their friends? Did that include Sally and her two bullish brothers? But why should they stop Hannah from enjoying herself?

She lifted her chin. "We'll be there. I'll bring one of those chess pies you like so much," she added, before Edith could ask.

"Good. I'll see you later." Edith gave a wave, the curls she took such pains to pin each night bouncing prettily against her cheeks as she flounced to the door.

Hannah frowned and fingered a lock of her own hair. How she wished for waves like Edith's, so pretty and thick and blond. She always looked like a ray of sunshine even on the gloomiest of days. Instead, Hannah's hair stayed stubbornly straight, no matter how much Liquid Silmerine she applied. And brown—not a pretty russet brown like Sally Bradshaw's. Hers was mousy and plain.

"Hannah? Is everything all right?" She startled at the voice at her shoulder and turned to see Mr. Smith with his hands on his hips, thin elbows jutting from his sleeve garters like two knobby twigs. "I called your name several times, but it was like you couldn't hear me." He pointed to the counter. "Your order is ready."

"I'm so sorry. I was just…" Hannah shook her head. No sense explaining. He already thought her a ninny. "Thank you, Mr. Smith."

He bobbed his grizzled head and turned to lead her back to the counter. "How are things out at your place? I noticed an extra sack of flour in your order. Your wheat crop looking all right?"

"Oh yes, it's fine. Pa says the wind laid some wheat down a few days ago, but it should recover by harvesttime."

"That's good to hear," Mr. Smith said. "Harvest is still a couple of weeks off." He patted the list Hannah had given him. "Let me know if there's anything else you folks need."

Hannah thanked him and, after paying him, slipped outside to where one of Mr. Smith's store hands had her wagon loaded and ready. She frowned, seeing it was Ernest Bradshaw. At seventeen years old, Ernest was lazy and tended to load the wagon sloppily. Still, it was better that she rearrange the supplies herself than to ask him to help and have to contend with another of his sly glances. And, more often than not when he helped with their order, Hannah found items were missing when she put everything away.

Catching sight of her, Ernest brushed his hands across his trousers and circled to meet her. "Hiya, Hannah. I thought I recognized your wagon. Loaded it up myself."

"Hello, Ernest." Hannah stifled a grimace at the bag of flour that threatened to topple a basket of apples. Pa would be angry if they arrived bruised. She shifted closer to the wagon. "I'm afraid I don't have a tip for you today."

The expectant smile slipped a bit, quickly replaced by the arrogant smirk Hannah found so irritating.

"That's all right. You can make it up another time." Stepping closer, he offered her a hand up onto the seat.

Another time? She wasn't sure she liked the sound of that. Instead of agreeing, she merely smiled, accepted his help into the wagon, and gathered up the reins. "Thanks again. Goodbye, Ernest."

"Bye, Hannah."

He moved to give room to the wagon as Hannah chirped to the mare, but she could feel his gaze lingering on her until she swung onto the street and rounded the corner to head out of town.

Shuddering, Hannah urged the mare into a faster clip. The apples and flour could wait, because the last thing she wanted was to spend one second longer than necessary under Ernest Bradshaw's uncomfortable stare. If that meant bruised apples, so be it.

Of course, eventually, she'd have to deal with him. The length of his glances was becoming increasingly improper. If she wasn't careful, she'd be the next topic for the gossips, a problem her father and Uncle Titus surely didn't need—not with business being so poor. The war made many afraid to spend what little savings they had—and who could blame them? It wasn't like anyone could know how long this troubling season would last or how bad it would get.

That last thought settled like a shroud over Hannah's shoulders and stayed firmly in place all the way home. No matter how hard she tried to shake it—she couldn't help but wonder.

How bad *would* it get? How long before the townsfolk of Panic let panic overtake them?

# Chapter Two

The sun had just crested midday—its rays hot on the top of Hannah's head—and was beginning to creep toward afternoon by the time she passed the wooden barn and outbuildings that edged her family's farm. No doubt Pa would be surprised to see her back so early, since trips into town were a treat she usually stretched out as long as possible. Not today, with the words about the Muellers burning her ears and the memory of Ernest Bradshaw's appraising gaze stinging her flesh. Today, it was the safe confines of the farm she longed for, with its quiet fields of golden wheat dipping and bending on an ever-present Pennsylvania breeze.

"Whoa, girl." Hannah pulled on the reins, slowing the mare so as not to stir up a cloud of dust she'd be sweeping from the porch later. That was one thing the weeks of no rain had garnered—endless piles of dust and dirt that accumulated on every stair, table, and shelf. Finally, she rumbled to a stop in front of the one-and-a-half-story house her father had built. It was where she and her brother had both been born…and where her mother had passed away just shy of five years ago. Even so, her touch still lingered in the trees whose spreading limbs offered welcome shade and the flowers whose cheery color welcomed her home.

Her father waited on the steps to greet her, a single sheet of paper fluttering in his hand.

"Hannah, I'm glad you're back. We've got a letter from your brother. Come." He beckoned to her, an excited smile on his face.

Hannah set the brake and looped the reins around the handle. "How? I was just in town, and there was nothing at the post office."

"Titus brought it by. Said it came in the post early this morning. You must have just missed him."

Hannah clambered from the wagon, the supplies forgotten as she rushed to join her father. "How is he? Did he say where he's writing from?"

"See for yourself." He handed the page to her. Snatching it, she devoured the words eagerly.

"France," she whispered when she finished. She shook her head. It was so very hard to believe that her mischief-loving brother was now thousands of miles from home, living in a country she'd only read about in books. Or that soon, he'd be fighting in a war she didn't fully understand. Suddenly, a knot of fear tightened in her belly thinking about it.

Her father's hand closed over her shoulder. "Don't fret, Hannah. It'll take a while to get the troops trained and ready to fight. Likely the war will be over before Silas even gets around to it."

His voice hitched at the end, and Hannah knew he was working hard to convince himself that what he said was true.

She nodded brightly and glanced up at him, his face blurring through her tears. "Yes, Pa, I'm sure you're right."

She folded the letter carefully and held it out to him. He declined it with a shake of his head. "You hold on to it. It's safer in your hands than mine."

Swiping the tears from her eyes, Hannah pressed the letter to her chest and motioned to the house. "I'll get the supplies unloaded then start on supper. Will you be in the fields long?"

"Not too long. Titus helped me with the livestock, so all I've got left is a few chores in the barn."

"Is he still here?" Hannah asked, squinting to search the barn's dim recesses for her uncle. "I can set another place at the table."

Adding a third person to their supper table was a common occurrence, since Titus often relied on her father for wisdom and advice. Hannah had long since started cooking for three just in case he showed up.

"No need. Said he had some errands to run before he headed home. Likely he'll stop for breakfast in the morning though. He needs my help sorting through his orders."

Again? Hannah fought the urge to roll her eyes. It was one mess after another where her uncle was concerned. As far back as she could remember, her father had been helping him out of his scrapes.

"...and then we've got some repairs to do on the thresher before the harvest starts," her father was saying. He braced one foot on the bottom rung of the porch railing and scratched his chin. "Also, I want to make sure the grain binder is ready to go before next week. Titus will help me see to that."

These were all things Silas would have helped with were he not serving his country on a foreign continent. Hannah felt a niggle of remorse for having thought badly of her uncle and gratitude that her father would not have to prepare for the harvest alone. But what about the other farmers? What would they do? Their sons had gone off to war too. Who would help them? Of course, they would help one another where they could. That was what people did in this small community. Or what they used to do.

Once again, the whispered words about the Muellers pressed on Hannah's heart. As her father swung toward the barn, Hannah started to call out to him then thought better of it. He had enough care on his shoulders without her adding more.

A sigh slipping from her lips, Hannah made her way inside to the small kitchen where she'd learned to cook by clinging to her mother's apron strings. Every item in here, every pot, towel, and wooden spoon, reminded her of her mother. Along with an oak table her uncle Titus had made for her parents as a wedding present, there were four ladder-back chairs, a pie safe fastened with punched-tin doors, and a large, black woodburning stove that had made her mother the envy of their town. In it, she had baked more loaves of bread than Hannah could count, prepared countless meals, and even dried socks on occasion.

Granted, many homes in Philadelphia and other large cities had electricity and running water. A few families she'd heard of even had telephones. But not in Panic. Most farmers here still depended on kerosene lamps and wells they dug themselves, the Walkers included, but Hannah didn't mind. There was a simplicity in the everyday tasks of lighting a fire in the stove and replenishing the water barrel that she found comforting, especially now, with the war looming over everyone's heads.

Hannah had just finished unloading the wagon and was putting a pot of water on to boil for the potatoes when a nicker from outside caught her attention. A glimpse through the kitchen window told her it was Edith. Judging by the bonnet bumping against her back as she dismounted and the loose tendrils of hair clinging to her cheeks, she was agitated. Hannah left the stove and went outside to meet her.

"Have you heard?" Edith asked before Hannah was fully on the porch. "Pastor Beech has called a meeting at the church and asked everyone in town to come."

A meeting. On a Tuesday? Hannah frowned. "I don't understand… Has something happened?"

Edith's eyes widened somberly. "Apparently, someone received a telegram."

The word hit like a blow to the stomach. In wartime, telegrams could only mean one thing. Hannah folded her hands over her middle. "Do we know who?"

Edith's horse pawed the ground nervously, as though sensing the emotion transferred from Edith's fingers on his neck.

Edith's voice dropped to a whisper. "Not definitely, though I did hear Harmon McDow's name mentioned."

"Not Joshua," Hannah whispered, picturing Harmon's son as she'd last seen him, blue eyes bright with excitement and a wide grin on his lips. She shook her head. "But how? Pa said our troops haven't even started fighting yet."

"I don't know, but we'll be at the church tonight." Edith's hand inched toward the pommel. "Maybe we'll find out something then. Will you come?"

Hannah nodded. "Of course. I'll let Pa know."

Edith spun and climbed up onto her horse, riding astride like a boy. "It starts at six," she said, gathering the reins. "Mother said the pastor wanted to give everyone time to call the men in from the fields."

"Can I help?"

Edith calmed her prancing horse and shook her head. "You were the last on my list. Everyone else has already heard the news. I'll see you there."

Her horse needed no coaxing to break into a canter back the way they'd come. Edith neared a rise and then disappeared in a cloud of dust, grass, and flashing hooves. Realizing she still clutched her hands to her middle, Hannah swiped her hands down her skirt and headed for the barn.

Joshua McDow was only slightly younger than Silas. He'd turned eighteen last November, and both Edith and Hannah had danced with him at the harvest festival to celebrate.

Only eighteen.

Eighteen.

The walk to the barn had never seemed so long. All the way, the image of Joshua's smiling face pounded through Hannah's brain. And another thought as well—one that made her sick to her stomach and brought red-hot tears to her eyes.

She hated that something bad might have happened to Joshua... but she was so, so glad it wasn't Silas.

# Chapter Three

Despite the empty seats where boys-turned-soldiers would have sat, it seemed the entire town of Panic had gathered at the church. Today there were no cheerful greetings, however, or smiling faces and pleasantries exchanged in the aisles. Instead, there were muffled whispers and shuffling feet as people filled the pews and eyes that didn't linger too long on any one person. Hannah understood why. They were all thinking the same thing she'd thought when she heard the news…at least it wasn't my boy. My brother. My son.

Clutching a worn hymnal, Hannah sank down onto a hard wooden pew. Pa had yet to join her. He lingered near the door, talking in quiet tones to a couple of neighbors.

In the very front row, Harmon McDow sat stiff-backed and somber, neither greeting nor being greeted. His reddish brows were bunched in a line, his jaw hard, his eyes blank and staring. Next to him, Pastor Beech sat with his head angled close, whispering something for Harmon's ears alone. Whether he heard wasn't clear. He hadn't moved an inch since Hannah and her father and Uncle Titus arrived.

Edith slid next to Hannah on the pew, her knee bumping Hannah's. "Did you hear?"

Hannah glanced at the people filling the pews around her, none of whom seemed to be paying any attention to them. "Someone said it was pneumonia."

Edith pulled a handkerchief from her sleeve and dabbed her nose. "Can you imagine? Going all that way to fight for your country, only to die of—"

Seeing a couple of gazes swing their way, Hannah nudged Edith into silence then returned the hymnal to the seat back in front of her. Finally, the shuffling quieted, and Pastor Beech braced both hands on his knees and stood to make his way to the pulpit. As good an orator as Pastor Beech was, Hannah didn't think she'd ever seen the people anticipate his every word the way they did now. As he opened his mouth to speak, she leaned slightly forward in her seat and felt everyone around her do the same.

"Thank you all for coming." Pastor Beech cleared his throat and motioned to the front pew. "Your love and support mean the world to me, as I'm sure it does to our brother Harmon."

Heads around the room bobbed, except for Harmon, who sat as though sculpted from stone. No one sat next to him, Hannah noted. It was almost as if they were afraid to get too close. Afraid his luck, or lack of it, would rub off.

Pastor Beech drew in a deep breath and gripped the pulpit with both hands, his gaze steady as he looked around the room. The color in his cheeks heightened the intensity that shone from his blue eyes, but the way his fingers shook as he beckoned the last stragglers in gave him away.

He waited until everyone was settled then began again. "This is a day I prayed would never come. I've feared it, as I know many of you have. I've prayed against it. Even railed against it." His eyes drifted to Harmon. "Foolishly, I thought I'd reconciled myself to the inevitability of it."

Here and there, sniffles started. Hannah didn't need to look to know who inspired the sounds—Alice Dawson, whose eldest had left to fight the same time as Silas. Mary Gordon—she and her husband had two sons gone to fight and a younger one still at home waiting his turn. The Andersons. The Cupits. The Randolfs…

The list was long. All friends. Neighbors. All sitting here, like Hannah and her father, sick with worry. Hurting for Harmon. Angry.

She startled at the last word and looked around. Each tightly clamped mouth, every moist eye and fisted hand, reflected the same emotions boiling inside her. Worry and hurt she could understand, but anger? Closing her eyes shut out the faces of other people, but it only intensified the feelings inside her. She hated the empty seats where friends should have been. She hated the way she scoured the road, fearing the plume of dust that signaled an unwanted visitor. She hated the war. She hated…

"Germans!" Harmon shot to his feet, shattering the stillness in a way that brought gasps from some of the women. "It's their fault our sons are over there fighting and dying. It's their fault the whole world is at war!"

Hannah sucked in a shocked breath. Around her, worried muttering buzzed, and then silence fell. Heads turned. Hannah shifted on the pew to see what they looked at. Not *what*, she realized, but *who*. Karl Mueller stood at the back of the room, his hat crushed in his hands, his cheeks red and his lips white. Niklas stood next to him, mouth slightly open, his hands clenched into fists at his sides.

Edith leaned in to whisper, "I can't believe they're here, considering what everyone is saying."

Hannah jerked her attention to her friend. "What are they saying?"

"Harmon." Pastor Beech's quiet voice turned all heads back to the front. He waited for the shuffling to quiet before he spoke. "Let's remember it's Germany we're at war with, not other Americans."

Harmon's mouth worked a moment, his hands opening and closing uselessly at his sides. Then, as quickly as it came, the burst of strength left him, and he crumpled onto the pew.

"Oh." Edith's hand rose to her mouth, a motion Hannah saw duplicated around the room.

"This will be a difficult time for all of us." Entreaty filled Pastor Beech's gaze as it swung over the room, lingering here and there. "We must remember to pray for one another. To encourage one another when we can. Bear one other's burdens. Most importantly, we must remember to treat one other with the grace and love we have been shown."

He went on, but his words confused Hannah. She'd expected him to talk about Harmon, or managing their fears, or how they could help the troops abroad. Instead, for several minutes, Pastor Beech spoke only about the acts of kindness he'd witnessed since coming to Panic. He talked of neighbors helping neighbors, of weddings, and baby showers, and funerals that had taken place in the room where they sat. Slowly, Hannah realized that what he was doing was urging people not to let the war rob them of one of their most precious possessions—their love and concern for one another. Fear could do that, she realized. Was already doing it…or at the very least, it was trying.

Slipping her hand over Edith's, Hannah squeezed, then with her other hand reached over to grasp her father's. To her surprise, his fingers were cold and rigid and his gaze was not locked on Pastor Beech as she expected. It was fixed over his shoulder on Karl Mueller.

"Pa?" Hannah angled her head toward him. "Are you all right?"

He turned his head and blew out a breath. "Yeah." Squaring his shoulders, he directed his attention to the pastor. Hannah did the same.

"For those needing help with your harvests, I've spoken with Henry Anderson. He's agreed to organize a sort of work exchange, if you will, for anyone who finds themselves shorthanded. Also—"

A hand shot up near the front of the church. "Pastor, if I may?"

Hannah craned her neck to see who spoke.

"Yes, John." Pastor Beech beckoned for John Taylor to stand.

"Oh, him." Edith crossed her arms, her lips curving downward in a disapproving scowl. "I bet he just wants to brag about how much money he has."

It was true, the Taylors were wealthy. John had made his fortune in real estate. Folks said it was the land that had brought him to Pennsylvania. Still, that didn't mean he wouldn't have something helpful to add.

"Edith, shush," Hannah scolded before turning her attention to what John was saying.

"Now, I know times are tough, what with the drain on food and supplies brought on by the war. We're all doing what we can, but there's no denying the shortages."

His gaze skipped to the back of the room and returned to the front. It wasn't a long glance, but it was enough to remind Hannah and probably others about the Muellers' presence.

"As a good neighbor, I'd be remiss if I didn't at least offer to help. After all, that's what neighbors do."

Hannah's brows rose in surprise. John Taylor wasn't known as one to lend a helping hand. In fact, more often than not—

"Which is why I am willing to speak with anyone who finds themselves in need of a small loan. Just to carry you through," he continued, raising his voice to be heard above the murmured groans. "I charge a modest interest, of course—"

The murmuring increased.

Pastor Beech lifted his hand. "Thank you, John."

"It's just sound business practice, Pastor."

"Yes, yes, I understand. Thank you."

Straightening the string tie at his neck, John retook his seat. Gradually, the whispers quieted.

"I'm sure we're a long way from needing loans," the pastor said, giving a nod to John, "but I appreciate your kind offer."

From the end of the pew, Uncle Titus spoke up. "Maybe not so long, Pastor. It's been nigh unto a month since our crops had a good soak." He looked at Hannah's father. "I know a storm now would be bad for your wheat, William, but with most of our able-bodied men gone off to fight, half the town is struggling to keep their crops watered."

"You don't have to tell me, Titus," her father answered. "There's worry enough for all of us."

Though he didn't mention her brother's name, Hannah knew he meant Silas. She slid her gaze past her father to her uncle Titus. The times when he and her father were at odds were rare, which only made the moment more uncomfortable.

"Indeed, you're right, William," Pastor Beech said, drawing the attention away from Hannah's family to himself. "But doesn't God tell us the answer to worry is found in His Word? Let us then take a moment to seek His guidance."

After retrieving his Bible from the pulpit, Pastor Beech rustled the pages then began reading from the Psalms. Plagued by sorrow and doubt, Hannah only half heard the words. The pastor could say what he liked, but the war had already claimed some of the peace and contentment that had once graced her humble town. Tonight was ample proof of that. For her, the real question was, would they ever get it back?

# Chapter Four

Pastor Beech had long since concluded the hastily called town meeting, but many people still lingered, both inside the church and outside on the lawn, where the chirp of crickets added to the hum of conversation. Most of the talk outside revolved around the crops, though every now and again, Hannah caught snatches of conversation that included strange words like "doughboys" and "Cantigny." To her left, cast into shadow by a large oak and the darkening sky, her father spoke earnestly with Henry Anderson.

"I've got the thresher working," Pa said, his hands shoved deep into the pockets of his trousers. "Once the harvest starts, I'll need at least two, maybe three days to clear my fields and bind my wheat. After that, you can count on my help wherever you need."

Henry was a burly man, second in size and heft only to Hannah's father. His lips stretching in a grin, he clapped his hand on Pa's shoulder. "Thank you for that, William. The people in this town can always count on you. I hope you know how much we all appreciate it."

"I'll help too." Stepping into a circle of light cast from the glow of wagon lanterns, Uncle Titus nodded to Pa. "I know Silas usually runs the grain binder, William. I won't be nearly as good at it as your boy, but I reckon I'll get the hang of it easy enough. I'll be glad to help out where I can."

Pa frowned, lifting one hand to rub his scalp. "Titus, are you sure? What about your business? Won't you have orders to fill?"

"What orders?" A snort rippled from Uncle Titus's lips. He never resembled Pa more than when he scowled. Though he was six years younger and nearly a head shorter, the lines gave him the same look of maturity her father owned.

"Folks have done their best, William, but dry as it's been this summer, the harvest will likely be a lot lighter this year." His scowl deepened. "Which, I suppose, is a blessing, considering there are no farmhands to bring in what crops do need harvesting. No crops means no money. No money means no new orders for my furniture." His eyes narrowed as he jammed both hands on his hips and growled, "I know you don't like to hear it, William, but I'm with Harmon on this. It's because of this war that we're in the straits we're in."

Hannah sucked in a breath. Here at least was one big difference between the two brothers—Pa didn't have nearly as quick a temper and didn't often rush to judgment the way Uncle Titus was wont to do. Still, Pa would soon set him to rights.

Only...he didn't. To her surprise, her father didn't say a word. Instead, it was Henry Anderson who spoke.

"Now, now, the war ain't got nothin' to do with the weather. Likely we'd be in the same straits even if President Wilson hadn't led us into this war."

Uncle Titus grunted in disapproval. "Maybe so, but we'd have a lot easier time of it if we had our boys home to lug water from the river," he continued doggedly. "But all that is beside the point. What I'd like to know is why Karl Mueller's here in the first place. He's a clockmaker, not a farmer. This isn't any of his business."

"He's as much a member of the town as you or me, Titus," Henry replied, his gentle answer belying his size. "Town business *is* his business."

"Well, that may be your opinion," Uncle Titus said, his voice rising sharply. "It isn't mine."

Instead of arguing with her uncle, Henry dipped his head in a way that could only be described as respectful. "I'm sorry to hear that, Titus. I truly am."

"And his boy is still here instead of off fighting," Pa added. "Seems to me, his presence here is bad form."

Hannah's eyes rounded in disbelief. Pa was normally the voice of reason at times like this. Never had she heard him speak ill of another or sound so harsh.

"Before we go criticizin' the choices other people have made, let's remember Karl Mueller has already buried two sons due to scarlet fever and a wife who died givin' birth to a third." Henry's large shoulders slumped. "I can't speak for him or his son, but I do know that family has suffered loss. Maybe it's time folks gave them the benefit of the doubt."

With each word, Hannah's estimation of Henry Anderson grew. He didn't seem to hold any ill will toward the Muellers. Neither did Pastor Beech. She frowned. So then, maybe Edith's estimation of what people were saying about the Muellers was wrong. Maybe it was only a handful of people who disliked or distrusted them and not everyone in town as she'd said.

Still talking, the three men eased farther into the shadows, their low voices gradually fading so Hannah could no longer hear what was said. Heaving a sigh, she determined to look for Edith. Maybe if she could figure out where the rumors were coming from, she could help put a stop to them.

Only it wasn't Edith's gaze Hannah met when she turned. It wasn't Edith who stared back at her with eyes large and wounded and even a bit accusing.

It was Niklas Mueller.

# Chapter Five

For several long seconds, neither Hannah nor Niklas spoke. Slowly, she lifted her hand to her throat. How long had he been listening? With the gloom pressing in from late evening, she hadn't even noticed him.

"Niklas…"

Her voice seemed to shatter the fragile stalemate between them. He turned and set off toward the wagons, his long legs adding quick distance. Skirts flying, Hannah followed.

"Niklas, wait." He gave no indication that he heard. If anything, his pace only increased. Hannah hurried her steps to match. "Niklas, I'd like to talk to you—"

She drew up short as he pivoted and strode back to her.

"Do you agree with them?"

In the failing light, she could barely make out his face, but there was no mistaking the anger in his tone.

"Your uncle and your father?" He lifted his hand to gesture furiously toward the church. "And everyone else in there who thinks like they do. Do you agree?"

"First of all—"

"Just answer the question, Hannah," he ground out, crossing his arms over his chest.

She sucked in a breath of sultry night air and straightened. "All right then...yes, I do agree."

Niklas's hands dropped to his sides and his mouth snapped closed.

"With Henry Anderson and Pastor Beech," Hannah continued quickly, "and everyone else who knows what a good man your father is."

Compassion swelled in her chest as she watched Niklas's shoulders slump. It had to have been hard for him to hear his family spoken of so, yet somehow he'd stopped himself from letting a fight break out and making the situation worse. Reaching out, she touched his arm.

"Niklas, not everyone thinks poorly of your family. That's what I'm taking away from all of this talk tonight. You heard the pastor. It's grace and love that are called for in these trying times. I, for one, think most people agree with him."

His head lowered, and he slid his hands into the pockets of his dark trousers. "Your uncle does not. Nor, by the sound of it, does your father."

"Pa is worried about Silas," Hannah said, feeling a bit defensive but helpless to stop it. Whipped by a warm breeze, a wisp of hair fluttered across her cheek. She tucked it behind her ear and leaned toward Niklas earnestly. "He never would have spoken so otherwise."

In Niklas's gaze was a wealth of hurt and bitterness. "You think my father and I do not worry? I've known your brother my whole life. I know all the men who've gone off to fight. If I could, I'd be right there beside them—"

He broke off, his jaw clenched and dark eyes smoldering.

*in Panic, Pennsylvania*

Something deep inside Hannah tightened at the thought of Niklas joining Silas and the others on the battleground. Swallowing hard, she grasped the sides of her skirt and managed a small shrug. "Some people are needed more at home. It doesn't mean their role is any less important."

"That may be true, but you have to admit, my being here while others are away only fans the gossip."

"Speaking of that—" Desperate to change the subject, Hannah motioned to the last few stragglers lingering around the church. "Have you seen Edith? I thought she might be able to help pinpoint who's been doing most of the talking."

Niklas narrowed his eyes. "Why?"

Hannah lifted her chin and crossed her arms jauntily. "Well, so we can put a stop to it, of course."

Scrubbing his fingers across the scruff on his cheek, Niklas shook his head. "You don't have to do that, Hannah. What people are saying about Papa and me is not your concern."

"You're our neighbors, aren't you? And Pastor Beech did say we're supposed to take care of one another, didn't he?" she persisted.

Slowly, the troubled lines cleared from Niklas's forehead. His lips even twitched a bit, as though tugged by a smile. "That he did. Thank you. My father and I... We appreciate your kindness." He paused, and his chest rose and fell with his deep breath. "*I* appreciate it."

Warmth melted over Hannah as she held out her hand to him. "Will you come with me to look for Edith? Maybe we can get to the bottom of these rumors."

He hesitated only a moment before his fingers closed around hers. Though it was purely a friendly touch, Hannah felt her pulse skitter. Did he feel it too? She slanted a peek at his stoic profile. His chiseled jaw darkened by the shadow of his beard. The raven-like swoop of his hair across his brow. If he did feel the same excitement that coursed through her veins, it didn't show.

Too quickly, they neared the lantern glow spilling from the church windows. Niklas pulled his hand away and angled his head toward the door. "I will wait here while you look for Edith."

Though she hated to leave him, she understood his reluctance to go back inside. She turned to reach for the railing. "I'll only be a moment."

Niklas nodded, but Hannah had only climbed one step before her father's voice stopped her in her tracks.

"Hannah?" As Pa approached, his gaze swung between her and Niklas. "What is this? Where have you been?"

"You were with the Mueller boy…alone?" Uncle Titus narrowed a suspicious glare on Niklas.

Hannah's throat suddenly went dry. "We were just talking, Uncle Titus. I told Niklas I would help him—"

"Hannah, please wait in the wagon." Pa's tone brooked no argument. Surely, he didn't think…

"It's late," he added more gently. "We should be gettin' on home."

Niklas stepped forward, his chin lifted and his shoulders squared. "Hannah is correct, Mr. Walker. We were just talking."

"Maybe so," Uncle Titus cut in before Pa could answer, "but it still isn't seemly for a young lady to go wandering off in the dark. Perhaps if you were a little more familiar with our ways, you'd know that."

"That isn't fair," Hannah protested. "Niklas has lived here his whole life."

"His father hasn't," Pa said, shocking Hannah into silence. Behind her, a new voice cut the sudden tension.

"Niklas, son, please gather our things. It's time we too were going." At the church entrance, Karl stood outlined in the lantern glow. Next to him, Pastor Beech observed everything quietly, an expression of concern creasing his face.

Niklas's face looked carved from stone. "Yes, Papa."

Though Hannah waited, Niklas did not glance her way. He turned toward the wagons and within moments was swallowed by the gloom.

Karl crossed to the stairs and moved to stand on the first step. "William. Titus."

He gave a nod to both, but only Pa returned it. Even then, it was grudging, with Pa refusing to meet Karl's eyes. Uncle Titus chewed the inside of his cheek, as though biting back words that threatened to spill from his lips. Had things always been so strained between her family and the Muellers? If so, why had Hannah never realized it before now?

Karl descended another step, his gaze fixed on Hannah's father. "Your wheat will be ready to harvest soon, *ja*? If my son and I can be of help, you need only ask."

"That won't be necessary," Pa answered, his tone curt.

For the first time in her life, Hannah felt the tiniest rush of embarrassment for her family heat her cheeks. And something else too. Something foreign and strange.

For the first time in her life, Hannah was afraid their way of life was changing—*people* were changing, marred by fear and bitterness. And deep down she knew...

Things in Panic would never be the same.

## Chapter Six

Hannah tossed and turned all night long, Pastor Beech's words chasing Pa's round and round inside her head. Though it would be several hours before the first hint of dawn pinked the sky, she slid from her bed and made her way to the kitchen to stoke the fire in the stove. The heat from the coals warmed her cheeks. She stirred them to life with a poker then added kindling and closed the door.

Normally, Thursday was her bread-baking day, but this week, she'd tackle the chore a day early and use her deliveries to seek out her neighbors. Maybe then she'd know who was behind the rumors circulating about the Muellers.

Soon, the scent of warm yeast filled the kitchen and with it, a measure of peace that had eluded Hannah ever since she'd heard her father speak against Karl Mueller. Granted, he'd only been stating a fact, but something in the hardness of his gaze had troubled Hannah and still did.

She crossed to the water barrel, ladled out enough for coffee, and set the pot on to boil. A short while later, her father's footsteps scraped the stairs and he appeared in the doorway, his shirt untucked and his hair still rumpled from sleep.

After taking a sip from the cup she offered, he sighed and settled heavily in a chair at the table. "You're up early." He glanced at the glowing oven. "Isn't tomorrow bread-baking day?"

Rather than explain, Hannah gestured to the window. "You're up early too. Do you have plans for this morning?"

He took another sip from his cup. "Thought I'd check the wheat on the south corner of the field. It gets more sun there. We might be able to start harvesting on that end."

Hannah bit her lip nervously. If Pa intended to start harvesting, she'd be needed here and not be able to make her deliveries.

Seeing the direction of her gaze, Pa set his cup down and shook his head. "Don't worry, it'll be at least a day or two. Even then we won't get too much done right at first. Probably a good thing you're filling your bread orders early, though, since I may need your help tomorrow or the day after."

A wave of guilt flushed her cheeks. She nodded and turned away to remove the loaves from the oven and insert two more.

She cut the heel off one and put the slice on a plate, slathered it with butter, and set it before her father. Seeing his cup was empty, she refilled it from the pot and then poured one for herself and settled in her chair.

Pa's finger tapped the side of his cup. "Something on your mind, Daughter?"

Hannah raised her eyes to meet his. Unlike Hannah and her mother, Pa had blue eyes and a reddish tint to his hair and eyebrows that Hannah envied. Though lines crisscrossed his brow and crow's-feet feathered the skin around his eyes, she had always thought him handsome. The signs of age had only given him an air of wisdom... or so she'd believed.

"Best speak your mind," Pa said, interrupting her troubled thoughts. "No good ever comes of keeping things bottled up."

Hannah pushed away her untouched coffee. "It's about last night."

"Figured so." He eyed her over the rim of his cup. "Is it the Muellers that kept you up tossing and turning, or something else?"

He'd heard her restless rustling? She sighed. "I'm worried for the Muellers, yes, but I'm also worried about what I see happening to the people in our town."

Pa's gaze fell to the contents of his cup. "People are always going to talk. Nothing much different there."

"But it's the way they talk. The way…you talked. Last night. To Mr. Mueller." The truth came in short, painful bursts. Fire licked up Hannah's neck to her cheeks. "Pa, why don't you like him?"

He didn't answer right away, and for a moment, she thought he wasn't going to. Finally, he lifted his chin and looked her right in the eyes. "Hannah, have I ever lied to you?"

She shook her head, tears gathering.

"If I tell you there are things between the Mueller family and ours that are better left unsaid, would you accept that?"

*What kind of things? And when did they happen? Did they involve her? Or Niklas?* These questions and more pounded Hannah's brain, but not one slipped past her lips. Instead, she nodded and hoped he'd say more. He didn't.

Once he'd finished with his bread and coffee, he deposited his cup and plate on the counter then grabbed his hat and boots and shuffled to the door. "Be back around lunch."

"I'll leave something on the stove in case I'm not done with my deliveries," Hannah said, quickly hiding her hands in the folds of her apron. Pa might not be willing to talk, but that didn't mean other people wouldn't.

Pa nodded then slipped outside, shutting the door carefully behind him. The moment he was gone, Hannah let out a sigh and set her full cup next to his empty one on the counter, all appetite gone, replaced by a knot in her stomach that refused to be quelled. When the last golden loaf finished baking, she wrapped each one in strips of cloth and stacked them all carefully inside a basket. With the horse hitched to the wagon, she set off, glad to leave the solemnity of the farm behind.

Daisy Cooper, a retired schoolteacher recently widowed, was her first stop. Though Daisy was good at many things and more educated than anyone else Hannah knew, she'd never learned to bake. As usual, Daisy was only too willing to chat. She brewed a pot of tea while Hannah told her about the meeting at the church house, her thin lips pinching into a line when she got to the part about Harmon McDow rising angrily to speak.

"It's a shame about his son," Daisy said when Hannah finished. "I remember having Joshua in my class when he was younger. Always a good lad and such a quick learner." She sighed. "But it would be an even worse shame if Harmon let his grief over his son turn him bitter toward others simply because they're of German descent."

"Unfortunately, that's a real possibility," Hannah said, drawing the sugar bowl near and spooning a tiny bit into her tea. Sugar was expensive, and she'd not take advantage of Daisy's small store. "And not just for Harmon. Other people have started to talk also."

Daisy's eyebrows rose. "What people?"

"I was hoping you could tell me." Hannah cradled her cup in both hands. "Daisy, have you heard anyone speaking ill of the Muellers?"

Daisy cupped her chin while she thought. "Honestly, I can't say I have. Of course, I don't get out as much as I used to." She tapped her finger against her skirt. "These old knees make it difficult to get around. Still, I find it hard to believe anyone could have something bad to say about Karl Mueller. That man has shown me nothing but kindness since he moved here, and his son has always seemed very polite." She paused to smooth a graying lock of hair over her forehead. "I never really knew his wife. We only spoke a couple of times, but she seemed nice."

Curiosity about Belinda Mueller stole priority in Hannah's thoughts. "I never got to meet her. She died before I was born."

Daisy's head bobbed. "Such a shame, that. She died giving birth to their third child."

"Niklas."

"Yes."

Hannah leaned forward to rest her elbows on the table. "Does he look like her?"

Daisy scratched her temple with her knobby finger. "Why yes, now that you mention it. She had the same dark hair and eyes. Such a lovely woman." Eyes twinkling, she fiddled with the handle on her teacup. "Many a man tried catching her eye, but she never spared a glance for anyone but Karl Mueller. Seems to me, her son will turn out the same way, seeing as he's well past marrying age. Guess he's just waiting for the right person to come along." She lifted her cup to her lips. "Of course, we don't know who the lucky woman will be who lassos his attention."

Unable to meet Daisy's gaze, Hannah fidgeted in her chair. The thought of any woman catching Niklas's attention left her feeling flustered and downright uncomfortable.

"How's your tea, dear? Would you like a refill?"

Hannah shook her head as Daisy held up the pot. "No, thank you. I really should be going. I still have several deliveries to make before I head back to the farm."

Daisy set the pot down and braced both hands on the table. "Speaking of your deliveries, will you be heading out past the Muellers' place, by any chance?"

"Oh…I…"

Daisy pushed up from the table and took several unsteady steps toward a pie safe huddled against the wall next to her kitchen sink. She swung the door open and pointed to a golden pie stored inside. "I made this yesterday afternoon with some cherries one of the neighbors brought me. I meant to give it to the Muellers as a thank-you for the firewood Karl delivered last week. But these knees…" She angled her head pleadingly at Hannah. "I would be so grateful if you could take it by—so long as it's not too far out of your way, I mean."

Hannah couldn't say no and found she didn't really want to, not if it meant seeing Niklas again. "I'll be happy to deliver it for you," she said.

A short while later, with the pie safely tucked into the basket on the seat next to her, Hannah made her way to the two-story house where the Davis family lived. Mrs. Davis was an exceptional baker in her own right, and Hannah had no delivery to make here, but she still hadn't spoken to Edith since last night and didn't want to miss the opportunity now.

Edith's pet beagle bellowed a warning as Hannah rolled the wagon to a stop. A moment later, Edith slipped out the door, a frilled apron tied around her waist and a cheery yellow dishcloth clutched in her hands.

"Hannah, we weren't expecting you today. Is everything all right at the farm?"

"Everything's fine," Hannah said, setting the brake before climbing down from the wagon. She looked toward the house, where a plume of smoke rose from the kitchen chimney. "Are your parents home?"

"Mother is, but Pa is feeding the livestock. Why?"

"Do you have a minute to talk?"

Skirt billowing, Edith spun, dropped the dishcloth over the porch railing, and called through the door, "Be right back, Ma. I'm talking to Hannah."

Her mother's response echoed from the rear of the house. "Don't be long."

"Come on." Edith took Hannah's hand and led her past the house toward the shallow pond where the two of them had played as girls. "What's going on? I didn't get a chance to talk to you after the meeting last night."

"That's why I came by," Hannah said. "I tried finding you, but I ran into Niklas Mueller instead."

Briefly, Hannah explained what had transpired and what had compelled her to make her bread deliveries a day early. "It's just not right for the Muellers to be treated so unfairly, Edith. Not when they've done nothing wrong. That's why I was hoping maybe you could tell me whose been filling your ears with rumors about them."

Edith listened quietly as she finished, displeasure tugging at her lips. "Well, I wouldn't say anyone's been filling my ears," she protested. "I mean, Sally Bradshaw may have commented once or twice—"

"I knew it," Hannah interrupted. "You know, Daisy Cooper said something today that makes me think Sally's attitude may just be sour grapes."

Edith frowned. "What do you mean?"

"Do you remember at the Christmas dance, when Sally made all that fuss about wanting to dance with Niklas?"

"Yeah."

"Well, Daisy said she thought Niklas was going to be like his mother. She only ever paid attention to Karl despite all the eligible bachelors in town vying for her eye."

"And you think Sally's been gossiping because she's still bent out of shape?"

"Well, wouldn't that be just like her?"

"Maybe," Edith said, though she didn't sound at all certain.

"Do you suppose there's a chance she's been talking to others besides you?" Hannah pressed.

"There's always a chance," Edith said. She grasped Hannah's hand. "But before you go running off blaming Sally, I should tell you something else."

Hearing the urgency in her friend's voice, Hannah paused. "Yes?"

Edith let go of Hannah's hand and straightened. "I know you don't trust Sally, but she's not the only one who's been talking, Hannah. I know you want to think it's no big deal, but it's more than just one person being jealous."

"What do you mean?"

Edith bit her lip and gestured to a large stone on the bank of the pond. When they were younger they used to jump from it into the water then lay on it baking until their clothes dried out. Smoothing her skirt, Edith claimed a corner of it now and made room for Hannah.

"I hung around after Pastor Beech ended the meeting last night," Edith began. "Several people did."

"I know. I saw," Hannah replied. "Pa and I stayed too. That's how I ran into Niklas."

Edith shook her head. "Sally's brothers were there. I heard them talking to a couple of the men from town."

Hannah let out a disgusted humph. "More Bradshaws. Figures. Everyone in that family has been known to gossip."

"No, Hannah." Edith grabbed her by the arm, her eyes widening solemnly. "They weren't the ones doing the talking. They were listening."

"What? So then, who was talking, and what were they saying?"

"It was John Taylor. I heard him mention something about money and land, and at first, I just thought he was bragging again, but then he brought up Karl Mueller's name."

Hannah shook her head in confusion. "What for? What did he say?"

Edith let go of Hannah's arm and pressed her palm to the stone. "I don't know exactly what was said, but I did hear him describe Mr. Mueller in less than complimentary terms. And right after that—"

She broke off and ripped her gaze from Hannah's.

Hannah leaned in close. "Right after that…what?"

Edith lowered her voice, the sound almost carried away by the trilling of goldfinches and rustling leaves stirred by the wind. "I heard him talking to someone else."

"All right." Hannah waited, and when Edith didn't immediately continue, prompted her with a poke from her elbow. "Edith, who was it?"

Edith dragged her gaze up, a hint of sorrow darkening her blue eyes. "It was your uncle Titus, Hannah. But not just him."

She didn't need to hear the rest to know what Edith would say, because she'd witnessed Uncle Titus last night with her own two eyes and knew who'd he'd been with.

"It was your pa, Hannah. John Taylor was talking to your uncle and your pa, and all three of them were discussing what it would take for John to get his hands on Karl Mueller's land."

## Chapter Seven

"Hannah, are you all right?"

Hannah blinked and drew her legs up on the stone to hug her knees. "You're sure you heard them say they wanted John Taylor to have the Muellers' land?" she asked weakly.

"Well, John was doing most of the talking," Edith said, "but your uncle seemed to agree with him. And if it makes you feel better, I got the impression both of them were trying to convince your pa."

"Of what?"

"I'm not sure, exactly," Edith admitted. "I'm sorry, Hannah." She grabbed Hannah's hand and squeezed. "Maybe I shouldn't have said anything?"

Hannah shook her head. "No, it's all right. Pa told me this morning that there's a history between our family and the Muellers. What it is, I have no idea, but maybe it's time I found out."

Edith angled her head curiously. "What are you going to do? Are you going to ask your father?"

"I will if I need to. First, I promised Daisy I'd deliver a pie to the Muellers." Hannah stood and brushed the dirt from her skirt. "Might as well start there." She paused and looked down at Edith. "Has there been anyone else talking?"

Edith shrugged. "If I know Sally at all, she's probably just repeating what she's heard someone else say."

So then, who was Sally listening to? Or was Edith wrong about Sally not being the one to start the rumors? Granted, Hannah didn't know Sally as well as Edith did, but there had always been something about the girl that didn't sit well.

Once again, a vision of Sally's beautiful russet locks raced through Hannah's brain, only this time, it was accompanied by a dimpled smile and flashing teeth. Oh, it wasn't so much that Sally liked to flirt that bothered Hannah. It was that, more than once, she'd seen her flirting with Niklas.

The realization slammed into Hannah with enough force to rob her breath. Lowering her head, she brushed a blade of imaginary grass from her skirt and then gestured back to the house. "I should get going before Pa wonders where I've been." She glanced over at Edith, who had gotten up and was busy shaking the dust out of her skirt. "You'll let me know if you hear anything else?"

"Of course," Edith agreed. "And if you want to stop by on your way home, Ma and I will have some fresh preserves for you and your pa. I know how much he likes elderberry."

"Thanks, Edith," Hannah said, turning to go.

"One more thing," Edith said, drawing Hannah's attention back. "Be careful. Around Niklas, I mean." Her mouth worked a moment, and then she shrugged helplessly. "I just don't want to see you drawn into that whole mess with his family. And Niklas is, well, don't let him turn your head."

Her cheeks flushed pink as she stumbled to a stop. Hannah nodded. She knew what Edith was trying to say. The problem was, Niklas Mueller had turned her head a long time ago. She'd just never been brave enough to admit it.

By the time the sun had crept high enough into the sky to warm the top of Hannah's head, she'd finished with her deliveries and was rounding the last bend in the road to the Muellers' farm. Patting the basket with the pie still tucked inside, Hannah slowed the horse to a walk. If she was honest, she'd been looking for a reason to speak with Niklas again, but now that she was here, she wasn't quite sure what she would say.

Both Muellers were in the yard when Hannah pulled to a stop, along with a giant dog who frisked about and lapped at the water flowing from a pump where Karl was preparing to wash up. Judging by the damp circles on Niklas's sleeves, he'd just finished. Leaving the pump, both men made their way over to the wagon, the playful dog at their heels.

Hannah swallowed nervously then reached for the basket. "Hello, Mr. Mueller. Niklas."

"Good afternoon, Hannah," Mr. Mueller said, a broad smile on his lips as he stopped to rest one hand on the horse's flank. He directed a snap of his fingers to the dog, who circled to sit obediently by his side. He then looked back up at Hannah. "What can we do for you?"

Standing slightly behind his father, Niklas swiped his hands down his pant legs to dry them.

"Daisy Cooper asked me to bring you this pie." She held the basket out. "She said to thank you for the firewood."

"Ach, a pie from Daisy Cooper is a welcome treat." He gestured to Nicklas, who stepped forward to accept the basket. "We were just washing up for lunch," Karl continued. "You are welcome to join us, if you like."

Hannah's gaze slid to Niklas, who looked up in time for their eyes to meet.

"I would like that very much," Hannah said softly, more to Niklas than to his father. After shifting the basket to his arm, Niklas held out his hand to help her alight from the wagon.

"Wonderful." Karl clapped his hand on Niklas's shoulder. "Will you take our guest inside while I finish washing up?"

"I will."

"Good. Come, Samson," he said, whistling for the dog.

He gave one last smile to Hannah and then turned and walked back to the pump, muttering softly to the pup. Left alone with Niklas, Hannah clasped her hands together nervously.

"I hope it's not an imposition that I stayed. I wanted to talk with you about last night."

She searched his face, hoping for a clue as to what he was thinking. At last, his gaze softened and he shook his head.

"It is no imposition." He held up the basket. "Shall we go inside?"

Holding out his hand, he allowed Hannah to precede him. The Mueller house, though not as large as some of the other houses in Panic, was well kept and neat, with a row of flower boxes that sprouted perennials on either side of a set of wide stairs, and green shutters that flanked all the windows. Though Karl or his son maintained them, Hannah imagined it was Mrs. Mueller who had insisted on the decorative touches, and she wondered for the second time that day what Niklas's mother must have been like.

Inside, the house was as neatly kept as outside, and once again, a few touches here and there—a bit of lace and a tiny, delicate desk in the hall—gave clues to a missing occupant.

"The kitchen is this way."

Niklas slid past her and led her down the wide hall to a doorway that split off to the left. There were no frills here, just a potbellied stove that showed years of use, pots that hung from hooks on the wall behind it, and a wide counter that stored jars of canned goods and tins for coffee, tea, and biscuits. The one piece of furniture that could be said to be extravagant was a beautiful oak table, polished to a warm, honey-colored sheen. Instead of being turned, each leg was shaped into a long, elegant wedge, wider at the top and narrowing toward the floor.

Hannah stepped forward to trace her fingers over the diamond pattern that ran along the edge of the table. "Oh my goodness, this is beautiful." She looked up at Niklas. "Did your father make this?"

He shook his head. "It belonged to my mother. I don't know where she got it."

On the wall behind her, a clock that must have been made in the Muellers' shop chimed the noon hour. Niklas left the pie on the counter to retrieve a platter from the icebox. "I hope cold ham is all right with you. Papa and I were just coming in from the workshop to grab a quick bite."

"Ham is fine. In fact..." Hannah crossed to the basket and took out one last loaf of bread wrapped in cloth. "I baked this fresh this morning. One of my customers is out of town, so I have extra," she explained. "Do you have a knife? I can slice it."

"Here." He set the ham on the table then crossed to a butcher's block on a shelf behind the stove and pulled out a bread knife. "Oh, and a plate." He took one from the shelf, handed both items to Hannah, and then stood next to her while she cut the bread into thin, even slices.

"We never got to finish our conversation last night," Hannah said as she sliced. She paused to glance up at him. "Niklas, I hope you know that whatever negative things anyone else might think or say, I do not feel the same."

He leaned against the counter facing her, his arms folded over his chest. "Thank you."

She resumed slicing. "I had a chance to do some investigating while I made my bread deliveries. A couple of people admitted they'd heard bits of gossip, but no one seems to know exactly who started the rumors."

She thought the news might be encouraging, but instead, Niklas frowned. After setting down the knife, she turned to him and laid her hand over his crossed arms. "Niklas, I don't believe there are as many people saying bad things as you think. Most people I talked to had nothing but good to say about you and your father."

"And the others?"

Hannah let her hand fall away. "It's the war that has them nervous and suspicious, not the two of you."

"And yet, someone is using that nervousness to stir up trouble, is that not so?" He shook his head and pushed away from the counter. "I do wish I knew who this troublemaker is. I would put a stop to their rumors."

His fists clenched, and Hannah had no doubt the means he'd like to use, though she hoped he wouldn't. "We'll figure out who is behind the rumors," she said gently, drawing his attention back to herself.

"We?" He turned to her, a bit of the tension draining from his features. "I do not remember anything bad being said about your family."

Hannah lowered her gaze in embarrassment. "Maybe not, but my family is responsible for some of the talk," she admitted glumly. Startled by the warm touch of Niklas's finger on her chin, she raised her eyes.

"You are not your uncle Titus or your father."

The way he searched her eyes was doing wild things to her pulse. What was he looking for? What did he hope to find? Finally, his hand fell away, breaking the spell, and still Hannah had to blink repeatedly to clear her thoughts. Needing something to busy her trembling fingers, she reached for the knife and resumed slicing.

"Speaking of Pa and Uncle Titus, I understand there is some kind of history between our two families. Do you know anything about it?"

His frowned and drew back a step, adding much needed space. "What kind of history?"

"Apparently, something bad that happened between them. At least, that's what I think Pa meant, though, to be honest, he didn't say much." Realizing she was rambling, she stumbled to a stop.

Niklas appeared to think a moment then shook his head slowly. "I've always known they didn't care for one another. I just thought it was a matter of a difference in personalities."

"That's kind of what I thought too."

Finished with the bread, she carried it over to set next to the ham on the table. Now that her heart rate had returned to normal, she could think clearly. Grasping the back of a chair, she said, "Do you think your father would tell us what happened between them?"

Niklas shrugged. "We could try, but Papa has never been one to talk much about the past. I've asked him many times why he left Germany to come to America, and he's never once told me."

It surprised Hannah to realize she'd never before considered there might be a reason. Another thought followed quickly on the heels of that one… What if he'd never come? Karl would never have met his wife, Niklas would never have been born—

Niklas left the counter to walk toward her. Though she tried, she couldn't take her eyes off him. "Whatever the reason, I'm glad he came," he said.

The distance between them lessened. Finally, he stood near enough for her to see a few small flecks of sawdust in his hair and on his forehead. Before she could stop herself, she lifted her hand and brushed them away.

"Me too," she whispered.

The creaking of the front door, followed by scuffling footsteps and scratching nails in the hall, had them springing apart.

"Is that fresh bread I smell?" Karl's jovial voice belied the knowing twinkle in his eye as he peered first at Niklas and then Hannah. He bent slightly to keep Samson in check with one hand. "You are the cause of this delightful odor?"

"I am." She ducked her head, suddenly shy and not solely because of the compliment to her baking. Had Karl guessed the moment he'd just interrupted?

"Manna from heaven," he declared, swiping the plate from the table and bringing it to his nose for a deep whiff. "Ach, I have missed the smell of my Belinda's baking day." He gestured to Niklas. "Fetch us some milk, Son. I will get the glasses."

A jar of sweet pickles finished off their feast. Pointing to a rag rug near the door, Karl directed Samson to lie down then pulled out a chair for Hannah. When they were all seated, he held out his hands to them. Hannah took one and then caught her breath when Niklas's fingers closed around hers so the three of them formed a circle.

Head bowed, Karl blessed the food then winked at Hannah and reached for a slice of bread. "So, tell me, how is Daisy Cooper? I have not been by her place in several days."

"Cheerful as always," Hannah said, passing her plate into Niklas's waiting hands. He cut a piece of ham and slid it onto her plate then cut another for Karl and finally one for himself. While they ate, Hannah told them about her deliveries, how the Andersons had a mare ready to foal, and that the Baxters had slaughtered a pig. She stayed away from any mention of the real purpose of her visit, a fact Niklas acknowledged with a squeeze of her fingers when she passed him the pickles.

How good it felt to have his gaze rest appreciatively on her, and how comfortable it was talking with Karl about everyday things, as though she hadn't just spent a restless night worried about everything from gossip at home to war oversees.

When they finished their sandwiches, Karl motioned to the pie. "And now we should sample some of Daisy's cooking, eh? Just to see if it measures up to Hannah's."

The chuckle that followed fanned the warmth in Hannah's face, but she cut the pie and dished out a slice for each of them before picking up her fork. "So, Mr. Mueller—"

"Oh, Karl, please." He patted her hand and smiled kindly then whistled for Samson. Instantly, the dog appeared at his side, panting expectantly. After breaking off a small bit of crust, Karl fed it to Samson.

"Karl," she corrected, "Niklas and I were talking before you came in." She glanced at Niklas. He nodded for her to continue. She cleared her throat and turned back to his father. "You've known my family a long time."

"That is true." His head bobbed as he scooped up a bite of pie and popped it into his mouth. Savoring it a moment, he sighed in contentment then wiped his mouth with a napkin. "I don't know, Hannah, your bread may have met its match in Daisy's pie."

"I've had the privilege of sampling her pie before," Hannah said, forking up her own bite. "It's no contest."

Laughter rumbled from Karl's throat, and even Niklas smiled.

Hannah swallowed her bite of pie and took a sip of her milk. "So, about my family. I suppose you met them when you moved to Panic? How long ago was that?"

"Hmm…" Karl wiped a few crumbs from his beard and scratched his head. "They were some of the first people I met when I moved here, oh, some thirty years ago now."

"That's a long time." Hannah angled her head, genuinely curious. "And you knew no one? What made you decide to stay?"

"Ach." The mischievous grin returned. "That is simple. It was a woman."

"Belinda Mueller," Hannah said, returning his smile.

Karl's eyes misted with nostalgia. "Only her name was Smith then. The first time I laid eyes on her, I thought she was the loveliest thing I had ever seen." He gestured to Niklas with his fork. "My son favors her. When I look at him, I can still see her smile."

Hannah slid her gaze to Niklas, whose face had gone ruddy under his father's compliment. "She must have been truly lovely," she said.

Niklas lifted his eyes to her, but only for a moment, before he cleared his throat and looked away. "So, Papa, what happened between you and the Walkers?"

Karl laid his napkin down carefully next to his plate of half-eaten pie. "What do you mean?"

Gone was the trace of playfulness that had colored his speech and manner, wiped as clean as the plate left by Samson on the floor. Niklas forged ahead anyway.

"As far back as I can remember, there's always been some tension between you. And now Hannah's father says there is a history. What history? What happened?"

"A history." Karl puffed out a snort, his fingers worrying a corner of his napkin. His face hardened. Samson seemed to sense the change and laid his giant head in Karl's lap. Karl moved to stroke his fur in response. "That is…a good way to describe it, I suppose."

To Hannah's surprise, Karl sounded a bit sad when he said it, as though he regretted the memories flooding him. Reaching for his pie, he pinched off another piece of crust and gave it to Samson, who gobbled it noisily.

That was it?

Hannah glanced at Niklas, who shook his head. Apparently, his father was no more inclined to talk about what had transpired between their two families than her pa.

She pulled her napkin from her lap and laid it on the table. "Well, I should probably get going. I promised Pa I would help with the harvest when I got back, and he will be wondering where I am."

"Your father's wheat is ready to harvest?"

Karl's question merely expressed interest, but remembering his offer of help, Hannah's stomach fluttered uncomfortably. "Um, I think so. He was going to check the field this morning and then finish with repairs to the binder."

She fidgeted a moment then reached for her plate. "I'll help wash up."

"No need," Niklas said, stopping her. "Papa and I can manage."

"Oh." Her gaze bounced between them, sad that their brief camaraderie had come to such an abrupt end. "All right then. I'd best be on my way."

Both men stood when she did, but after saying her goodbyes, only Niklas followed her outside.

At the wagon, she turned to look up at him. "Niklas, if I said something to upset you or your father, I'm very sorry."

"Not you," he replied, though any trace of softness had left his gaze. "Your words are just a reminder, that's all."

"A reminder of what? Niklas?"

She searched his face, but he refused to look at her as he offered her a hand up into the wagon. Finally, she had no choice but to accept it. Settled on the seat, she took up the reins and looked down at him one more time.

"I'll keep trying to figure out who is behind the rumors spreading around town," she promised, but Niklas shook his head. When at last their eyes did meet, his were stony and hard.

"I'd prefer you did not."

"Why?" she demanded.

"Because your father doesn't like me. Never has. Whatever happened between our families, it is clear neither side has forgotten or forgiven."

Stepping back from the wagon, he stared up at her, his face as resolved and unmovable as ever she'd seen.

"Goodbye, Hannah."

Without another word, he turned and walked away.

# ∽ Chapter Eight ∾

Hannah was surprised to see several wagons lined up near the barn as she rode into their yard. Along with Uncle Titus's, there were two more and another horse chomping grass at the hitching pole. Most surprising was the presence of John Taylor's shiny Model T. As far as she knew, he was the only person in three counties who could afford one, but what was he doing here?

Grabbing her basket, she scrambled from the wagon. She hadn't been expecting company. Sometimes she'd make meals for the workers, but that was usually not until the harvest was in full swing. And anyway, it didn't look like any work was underway. There were no voices coming from the barn, no horses being hitched or wagons readied for binding.

Voices drifted to her as she approached the house—tense voices that immediately set her on edge. She reached for the doorknob, entered quietly, and deposited her basket in the kitchen before making her way to the living room, where the voices were coming from.

"It doesn't matter how long the parts take to get here from New York, Henry," Uncle Titus was saying, his face red and one hand waving in irritation. "Whether we can get it in time for the harvest is not the question."

"No, it's not," Harmon McDow growled. "The question is where the original part went and why anyone would see fit to take it." His scowl traveled over the faces of the seven men gathered around, all of whom Hannah recognized. They were all neighbors and farmers. Straightening to his full height, Harmon puffed out, "I think I know the answer."

From his seat near the fireplace, Pa looked up. "Now, Harmon, let's not go making accusations."

"You're too lenient, William," Harmon snapped back, leaning forward to point his finger at Pa. "You know as well as I do that there's one person in this town who has better reason than any of us to try and sabotage our crops. We'd all be better off without them."

Sabotage? Hannah pressed against the wall, out of sight of her pa but still within earshot. What on earth had happened while she was gone?

"We don't know it was sabotage," Pa insisted. "I'm missing a part to my binder, that's all. It could just as easily have fallen out after the harvest last year."

"What about my shaker?" Sam Prescott demanded. "It was perfectly fine when I stored it last winter."

"Or my tools?" asked Jonas Hutchins. "I'm missing several things I can't afford to replace. Not with the crops looking so poorly. What am I supposed to do?" The desperation in his voice reached a strident level.

"You don't think it odd, William, that several farms around here suddenly have tools missing and equipment broken?" Harmon continued. "Because I sure do, and I don't think it's a coincidence."

"What are you saying, Harmon?" Uncle Titus spoke up from the opposite side of the room.

"What I've already said," Harmon barked. "That I think Mueller's roots here may not be as deep as he claims."

A growing pit opened in Hannah's stomach.

"Well then..." John Taylor's voice broke the awkward silence that followed Harmon's declaration. "I suppose we can continue speculating about where the tools have gone, or we can do something."

Compared to the others, Mr. Taylor's voice sounded completely calm and reasonable. Or so Hannah thought. His next words dispelled her momentary relief.

"Any of you here brave enough to act?"

"I say we head on out to the Muellers' and search his shop," Uncle Titus said.

Before she could think better of it, Hannah pushed from the wall and spun toward the living room. "Pa, could I speak to you a moment?"

Her father's eyebrows lifted in surprise. "Hannah, when did you get home? I didn't hear the wagon."

"Just arrived." She motioned over her shoulder toward the kitchen. "I need to talk to you."

Pa moved to rise, setting off a ripple of disapproving looks and sighs.

Uncle Titus stepped forward and grasped his arm. "William, whatever it is can wait. This is more important."

For a split second, Hannah feared her father would listen to Uncle Titus, but then his gaze locked with hers. "I'll only be a moment."

More sighs followed, and a grunt or two accompanied by the toss of hands in the air, but Hannah ignored them and led the way to the kitchen.

"What is it, Hannah?" her pa asked, rounding to face her, both hands propped on his hips. "As I'm sure you heard, we're in the middle of a very important discussion."

The fact that she'd been caught eavesdropping should have warmed her cheeks, but she had no time for embarrassment when Niklas's and Karl's reputations were on the line.

"Pa, you don't really think the Muellers stole the tools those men are missing, do you?" She grabbed his arm in both hands and peered earnestly at him. "The Muellers have lived in Panic for years, and no one would ever think to accuse them of such a thing."

"That's true, Hannah, but the country has never been at war with Germany before either."

"I don't see what one thing has to do with the other," she pressed, clutching his arm tighter.

"The Muellers are German, Hannah," Pa said, the patience in his voice thinning.

"So are we, at least on Mother's side," Hannah protested.

"Your mother's ancestors came to America long before you were born. Long before your mother or I were born," Pa said.

"And? What does it matter if people have lived here one generation, or three?"

"That's enough, Hannah."

The edge in her father's tone sliced through her protests. He reached for her hand, but she pulled away before he could take it. A sigh rumbled from his chest.

"There are things happening that you don't understand. To be honest, I'd hoped never to have to explain it to you, but here it is…

We're at war. And that means fighting battles at home that are just as real as those in Europe."

"The Muellers didn't take any tools, Pa."

"Well, I certainly hope you're right," he said, turning to go.

Hannah shook her head. "No, Pa, I mean, I know they didn't. I was there. I stopped by their place after I finished with my deliveries to drop off a pie that Daisy Cooper made."

"You were supposed to come straight home after making your deliveries."

Seeing the angry look that crossed his face, she swallowed hard. Angry or not, she had to tell him the truth.

"They invited me to stay for lunch. I was inside their house, Pa. Even if they could have taken the tools, even if they waited until everyone had gone to bed and snuck around the countryside late last night, I would have seen something. But I didn't."

She trailed off, certain she'd proven their innocence, even if it earned her father's displeasure.

"So, your assumption is they would have just left those things in the open for anyone to see, is that it?" Pa crossed his arms and looked at her with more condemnation than she'd ever felt from him.

"Well, no, but—"

"Were you in their shop? Did you look around their land or inspect their wagon?"

"Pa." Tears threatened at his cutting tone. Still, he pressed on.

"I'm disappointed in you, Daughter. I've never known you to be disobedient or devious before today, but after what I've learned..." His scowl deepened. "I can only assume it's the Muellers' influence that has made you so."

"No, that's not it at all," she started, and then she stopped. What excuse could she give? He was right. At least, about part of it. She lifted her chin, despite the misery clogging her throat. "It's not the Muellers' fault. I knew you said to come home, but I wanted to stay. And I was the one listening outside the door a moment ago, not Niklas or Mr. Mueller."

She didn't think her father could be more disappointed in her or that he could look more heartbroken than when she'd told him she'd been at the Muellers'. She was wrong.

He said nothing as he stared at her, which made the hurt she read in his eyes all the harder to bear. Heaving a sigh, he left the kitchen, letting the door quietly close behind him.

As if the strength had suddenly gone from her legs, Hannah sank into a chair at the table. How could the day have turned into such a disaster?

She gazed out the window, hoping to read an answer from the Lord in the clouds dotting the sky. But it wasn't clouds she saw rising from the dirt road that led to their house. It was her worst nightmare.

It was a swirling plume of dust.

## Chapter Nine

Somehow, Hannah managed to make her feet move out of the kitchen and down the hall. There was no talk from the living room now, the angry chatter silenced by shocked looks as men gathered at the windows to watch her father walk outside.

Dimly, Hannah registered the open door. Uncle Titus on the porch, his face pinched as though he'd just hit his thumb with a hammer. Pa, his back stiff and straight as he accepted the yellow slip of paper the telegram girl from the post office in Altoona held out to him.

"Telegram for Mr. Walker," the girl said, the brass buttons on her sweater gleaming in the golden sunlight. "Will there be a reply?"

Seconds ticked by.

"Forgive me, sir, but I have several deliveries to make—"

"No reply."

Hannah had to strain to hear her father's words. Easing past Uncle Titus on the porch, she went to stand next to him. Both watched as the girl climbed back into the post office vehicle and set off the way she'd come.

For several interminable moments, neither moved. Finally, unable to stand it any longer, Hannah looked up at him. "Pa?"

He blinked from his trance and lifted the telegram, his hands shaking as he unfolded the slip of paper and read silently.

"What is it?" Hannah begged, chest near to bursting. "Is it Silas?"

Without a word, he passed the telegram to her and then whirled to look at Titus. "Gather up the men. We're going to the Muellers'."

Barely able to see through the tears blurring her eyes, Hannah scrubbed her hand over her face and tried again.

A row of numbers and letters lined the top of the page, along with the date. Hannah skimmed past them to the body of the message.

*Sincerely regret to inform you 14737 Private Silas P. Walker officially reported wounded. Will send further particulars when received.*

The telegram finished with just a last name. Silas's commanding officer, perhaps? Silas was wounded. How badly? Would he live?

She stared at the slip of paper, willing answers to appear that it refused to give. Uncle Titus and several others swept by, shaking her from her stupor. They were going to the Muellers'? No. Many of them climbed into their wagons and set off in different directions. It took a moment for Hannah to realize why.

The telegram girl said she had *several* deliveries to make.

Instantly, she began praying that the messages the girl carried wouldn't devastate people she loved. She prayed for the soldiers whose names the telegrams bore. For the parents, sisters, and brothers who watched fearfully as the telegram girl arrived at their door.

But Pa and Uncle Titus...

Both climbed into the wagon grim-faced. Tucking the telegram into the waistband of her skirt, she started toward them, intending to ask to go along, then stopped.

The other mare was in the barn. If she cut across the Andersons' field, she could beat Pa and Uncle Titus to the Muellers'. Not that she thought them guilty, but with the mood Pa was in, who knew what he might say or what could happen? At least Hannah could warn Niklas and Karl about the telegram. Maybe then they'd be a little more understanding if things got heated and Pa said something he didn't mean.

Hannah darted into the barn, got the horse saddled and ready, and set off at a gallop. Though the wind stung her face and whipped the tears from her eyes, she pressed on, urging the mare faster and faster until she spied the roof of Karl's shop. Only then did she slow enough to catch her breath. And only when she'd skidded to a stop did she pause to consider what her pa would say when he found out she'd come.

Seeing her coming, Niklas had broken into a run to meet her. He grabbed hold of the bridle and soothed the huffing mare then turned to her. "Are you all right? What is it?"

"My pa and uncle Titus are on their way," she said breathlessly. "There are tools missing from some of the local farms."

"And they think we took them?" he demanded angrily.

"They suspect you might have," Hannah replied as Karl joined them, hating the words even as she spoke them. "And then we got this today, which only made matters worse."

She yanked out the telegram and showed it to them.

"Coming on the heels of this?" Karl ran his hand through his gray hair then gave the telegram back to Hannah. "Your father is angry and needs someone to blame. Thank you for the warning, Hannah, but you should go."

She hesitated. "But…"

"I will take care of your father. Do not worry," he added gently, urging her toward her horse. "Go on home now."

Much as she wanted to stay, Hannah knew he was right. Her presence here would only make things worse for the Muellers. Still, she hesitated as she reached for the pommel.

Suddenly, Niklas was beside her, his hands firm and strong on her waist. "Let me help."

She held her breath as he lifted her up, his hand still on her knee until she was settled safely in the saddle.

"Be careful riding back," Niklas said, his voice low. "The mare is winded, and you don't want her to stumble."

"I'll be careful."

The moment stretched into two. Three. And then Niklas patted the mare on the rump and stepped away. Twisting to look over her shoulder, Hannah saw him lift his hand in a wave. She waved back, but jostled by the mare, she faced front until she'd regained her balance then looked again.

Niklas still watched her, his hands in his pockets and his shoulders slightly slumped. The look on his face broke her heart.

## Chapter Ten

Hannah paced the floor and checked the time on the mantel clock. Despite the fact that the span since she'd last checked felt like an eternity, only ten minutes had passed. Where were Pa and Uncle Titus? Night had fallen in earnest now, and still there was no sign of them. What had happened after she left the Muellers'?

She crossed to the stove, took a slender piece of kindling, and lit a kerosene lamp. The loaf of bread she'd cut for her and Pa's breakfast still sat covered on a plate. It seemed like days since she had baked it. Could it really have only been that morning?

Her stomach rumbled, but Hannah dared not eat, not with her nerves a jumble in her belly. She resumed pacing, her ears straining at every sound until, finally, she plopped into a chair. On the table at her elbow sat her father's Bible. Hannah grabbed it and hugged it to her chest.

"Lord, please work things out. Please let all of this turn out all right. Heal Silas, Lord, and bring him home to us. Please let Pa—"

The rumble of a wagon cut short her prayer. Hannah jumped to her feet, dashed to the window, and pulled back the curtain. She could just make out the dim outline of a wagon and the two men inside it coming down the road.

"Finally!"

She hurried to the door, threw it open, and stepped out onto the porch, but instead of pulling up to the house, Pa circled the wagon around to the barn. Of course he'd want to get the horse rubbed down and settled before he came inside.

To busy herself while she waited, she returned to the kitchen and put a kettle on to boil in case Pa wanted coffee or tea when he finished. Would he and Uncle Titus be hungry? Certainly. She grabbed the bread and some butter and set them both on the table with a small jar of strawberry jam. By the time the door finally creaked open, her nerves were as taut as the strings on a violin.

She looked up, but it was only Pa who entered. "Where's Uncle Titus?"

"Gone home." Pa crossed to the table, pulled out a chair, and sank into it wearily.

Hannah walked to the cupboard for a mug. "I'm heating some water. Would you like some tea?"

It wasn't the question she wanted to ask, but she knew her father well enough to know he'd speak when he was ready and not before.

"Tea would be good."

She grabbed the tin and shook the tea leaves loose before scooping a spoonful into the kettle. Once they'd had a chance to steep, she poured a cupful through the strainer, carried it to the table, and set it at his elbow.

"Thank you." He took a sip then wiped his sleeve over his mouth and looked at her. "I suppose you've been waiting up to talk to me."

She slid into the chair opposite him. "What happened, Pa?" she asked. "Did you talk to the Muellers?"

"I did." He turned to brace his arms on the table, his large hands engulfing the mug. "They agreed to let us look through their shop."

"And?" She held her breath, waiting for his reply.

"There was nothing there."

"Of course not." Propelled by relief and joy, the words burst from her lips. Too elated to sit, she pushed up from the chair and spun in a half circle. "I knew you wouldn't find—"

"They were in the cellar, Hannah," Pa interrupted, his brows forming a stormy line across his brow.

Hannah stumbled to a stop, unsure she'd heard correctly. "What?"

"The missing tools and the part for my grain binder... We found them in the Muellers' cellar."

She shook her head hesitantly then turned, paced, and turned back. "That can't be right. Someone else must have put the tools there."

"That's what the Mueller boy said," Pa replied.

"And you believed him, right?"

Pa shook his head in disgust. "Hannah, you know how ridiculous that sounds."

"No more ridiculous than Niklas or Mr. Mueller stealing tools from their neighbors," she insisted hotly. "Why would they do that, Pa? What would they have to gain?"

"You don't know?" Pa's palm slapped the table. "How many times do I have to say it, Hannah? They're German. They're doing everything they can to keep us from sending food and supplies to the boys off fighting." He jabbed his finger on the tabletop, punctuating every word. "We are at *war* with them, Hannah."

"No, Pa, we're not. We're at war with Germany." Though her knees shook, still Hannah found the strength to keep going. "The Muellers aren't Germany."

Pa shot to his feet, making Hannah's legs quake harder. "You can say that after today? After what happened to your brother?"

"Of course I'm worried about Silas, but that has nothing to do with Karl and Niklas."

His eyebrows rose at her use of their Christian names.

"The Muellers aren't responsible for Silas getting hurt," Hannah said, rephrasing her words.

"All right, that's enough, Hannah." He ran his hand over his chin wearily. "The fact is, we found the tools in their cellar. That's all there is to it."

"No, Pa, it's not."

"Hannah."

She ignored the warning on his face and forged ahead. "Someone has been spreading rumors about the Muellers all week. Now this. Obviously, someone is trying to make them look bad."

"That makes no sense."

"Neither does the Muellers stealing. Pa, I think someone wants to run them off. You heard Harmon McDow today. He practically admitted—"

"Enough!" Pa shouted, loud enough to cause Hannah to stumble back. He'd never raised his voice to her in such a way before, or stared at her with so much anger.

"I'll hear no more about it, do you understand?"

Hannah clamped her mouth shut and lowered her gaze.

Huffing out a breath, Pa turned and made his way to the stairs. "Make sure you blow the lamp out."

Somehow, she managed a nod. She and Pa had never fought like this. It made her sick to her stomach that they did so now. As his footsteps faded up the stairs, she crossed to the lamp and lowered the wick, realizing that there was still one more question she hadn't asked. One that left her feeling more weak-kneed and anxious than ever.

What would happen to the Muellers now?

## Chapter Eleven

When Hannah got up the next morning, the sky outside was as gray as her mood. Even so, Pa's bed was made and his coat and hat were missing from the coatrack in the hall. She hadn't even heard him stir. Hurrying through her washing up, she pinned her hair away from her face then changed into a plain cotton dress before slipping out the door.

In the barn, one of the horses munched hay in her stall. The other was gone, along with the wagon, which Pa only took if he was going into town. Though she knew he would disapprove, Hannah saddled the other horse and set off for the Muellers'.

This time, no dog romped outside. No smoke rose from the chimney. The house looked dark and quiet. Too quiet. Hannah slowed her horse to a stop then slid to the ground.

"Hello?" she called, cupping her hand to her mouth. "Anyone home?"

"You shouldn't be here, Hannah."

She turned at the sound of Niklas's voice coming from the shop. Dark stubble covered his chin, and his eyes were bleary and red-rimmed, as though he hadn't slept a wink. Though he was dressed, his shirt was rumpled and one tail was untucked. There was no sign of Karl.

"I came to check on you," Hannah said, looping her horse's reins over the hitching post. "Pa told me what happened."

Niklas's face flushed to a deep, ruddy hue. "Even more reason why you should go."

"Go?" She widened her eyes in disbelief. "Niklas, we have to find out who put those tools in your cellar."

His jaw worked, and his arms fell to his sides. "Then…you don't think…"

Hannah walked toward him, her heart in her throat at the look in his eyes—half hopeful and pleading, half wary and angry.

"Of course I don't. There's no way you or your father would have taken those tools, war or no war. But someone did, and we have to find out who."

Standing before him, she reached for one of his hands and held it between both of hers. "Why don't we go inside and talk to your father? Maybe he'll have an idea of where we should start."

Niklas shook his head. "He's not here. He went with your father and Titus into Brookville last night, after they found the tools."

"Why would they go—" Her heart skipped a beat. "The police?"

Niklas nodded. "Probably by now, word has spread about what happened. It's likely no one will even talk to us, let alone help us figure out who really took those tools." He moved closer, letting go of Hannah's hand to grip her shoulders. "I don't want you dragged into this, Hannah."

"You're too late," she whispered, her breath catching at his nearness. "I'm already in it."

"No." He shook his head.

"It was Uncle Titus who suggested searching your place, and Pa went along with him." Niklas's touch was warm on her shoulders.

She reached up to rub her hands lightly over his arms. "I have to do something, Niklas. You have to let me help."

And then, before she really even knew what happened, she was in his arms. Work in the shop had made his hands strong, his arms and chest thick. Breathing deep, Hannah pressed her face to his shirt, fighting back tears in order to savor this brief moment of heaven. Circling her arms around his waist, she squeezed. Felt him squeeze her in return. All too quickly, he pulled away.

Trying to calm her racing heart, Hannah pressed her palm to her chest.

"Let's go to the shop," Niklas said, a curious tremor to his voice. "We can talk about what to do next there."

The house would have been more comfortable, but as always, he was careful of her reputation, and she loved him for it. Inside, the shop was as neat and orderly as the house, though it lacked any feminine touches. On one side, lumber lay stacked and ready to be sawed, sanded, and fashioned into clocks. On the other side sat a bench with mechanical gears and parts sorted by size. Files hung from hooks, along with chisels, wrenches, hammers of varying sizes, pins, springs, and numerous other gadgets whose use Hannah could only guess.

Still, it was the finished clocks that captured her attention. Never had she seen so many in such varying styles. Tall clocks, ornate clocks, simple clocks with faces larger than her hand. Some were the color of golden honey. Others were dark and shone enough for her to see her reflection. All of them had one thing in common—a gentle ticking that spoke of passing time.

"They're so beautiful," she whispered. "I had no idea your father was so talented." She looked over her shoulder at Niklas, who watched her from the door. "You helped make these?"

He nodded. "I do most of the woodwork. Papa handles the clock mechanism and fits the glass."

Armed with this knowledge, she traced her finger over the whorls that scalloped the edge of one of the tallest clocks. Knowing Niklas's hands had been here, that he'd labored and sweated over each piece, filled her with admiration…and something else. Something deeper that spoke to her soul.

She sensed when he neared. Without looking, she knew he stood at her back—not touching, but close.

"You like it?"

She nodded. "I do. Your designs are absolutely amazing." She reached out again to touch the clock with the tip of her finger. "What kind of wood is this? I've never seen anything like it."

"That's because it's lindenwood. It grows in the Black Forest in southwestern Germany." He reached around her to take her hand and lay it gently against the side of the clock. "Do you feel that?"

"It's smooth."

"What else?"

She closed her eyes to focus her senses on her hand. "Warm."

He let go of her hand, and when she turned to face him, he said, "Lindenwood is best for carving the larger clocks because the grain doesn't split or run. But it's costly to ship. We only make a few of these a year."

"And the others?" Hannah asked, mostly because she wanted to stretch the intimacy of the moment.

"Black walnut, maple, pine." He shrugged. "It depends on the customer and the look they want to achieve."

He moved to another clock, this one for a mantel, perhaps, and beckoned her close. He flipped the clock over and pointed to a crown stamped into the wood. On one side of the crown was the letter *K* and on the other an *N*. Beneath the crown was an *M*.

"For Karl and Niklas Mueller," Hannah said.

He nodded and ran his thumb over the symbol absently.

"Does everyone leave their mark on the things they make?"

"Not always. Craftsmen like Papa, usually." At the mention of his father, his expression sobered.

"Niklas, we'll figure out who did this. Your father is innocent. We just have to prove it."

"How?" He set the clock down with a heavy sigh. "It's as I said. No one will speak with us."

"I'm sure that's not true. We just have to keep looking until we find someone who will."

She crossed to a desk where a pencil and pad of paper lay. She sat down in the chair and said, "Harmon McDow was one of the people at the house yesterday. So were John Taylor and several others." She jotted the names then turned the pad for Niklas to see.

"What is this?" He frowned.

"These are the people who had items stolen from their farms." She drew a line down the middle of the paper and copied Harmon and John's name on the other side. "And these are the people who might have had a reason to want to frame your father."

"Harmon I can understand. He is angry about his son's death. But John?" Niklas's eyebrows rose.

Swallowing hard, Hannah told him about the conversation Edith had overheard. "John would like nothing more than to get his hands on your land," Hannah said. Then she grimaced. "And as long as we're jotting down suspects, I suppose I should add Uncle Titus and…"

She shook her head. "No. I just can't believe Pa would do something like this."

"Leave him off."

She blinked back hot tears to look up at him.

His hand closed over hers. "I do not believe it either. Besides, there are other people with more likely cause."

Gratitude filled her at his kindness. Finished with the list, she held it up. "All right then, what do we do with this information? Where should we start?"

"Maybe your friend Edith can help? She lives near a couple of these farms. Maybe she saw something? At the very least, I'd like to hear for myself what John's plans are for our land."

"It's worth a try." She folded the paper and tucked it into her sleeve then stood. "Let's go."

"But…your pa?"

She turned for the door. "If he went to Brookville, it'll be at least this afternoon before he gets home."

Niklas agreed. It took only a few minutes for him to saddle a horse, and before long, they were on the road to the Davis farm. Not until the house was within sight did Hannah stop to wonder what kind of reception they might receive. What if the Davises had heard about what transpired the night before? Would they turn Niklas away? Would Edith turn *her* away?

She shifted in the saddle. "Niklas, if you're right and there are people who've heard about the robberies…"

"You think it would be better if I stayed behind?" He set his jaw in a mutinous line.

"Not behind," Hannah corrected quickly. "I think having you along would be good—it would show people you've nothing to hide—but it might be wise if I do the talking."

That, at least, he could agree to, so when they arrived at the farm, it was Hannah who knocked on the door while Niklas lingered near the horses. After a moment, Edith answered, her gaze immediately sliding past Hannah to where Niklas waited.

"So, you've heard?" Hannah asked.

Edith slipped out onto the porch and shut the door behind her. "It was all anyone talked about at the quilting circle. Hannah, what is he doing here?"

"*We* are trying to figure out who actually stole all those tools," she said, pulling Edith's attention back to herself. "Do you have a minute to talk?"

"Only if my father doesn't know you're here." She cast a quick glance at the barn and then beckoned for Hannah and Niklas to join her around the side of the house. "What do you want to know?" she asked, crossing her arms over her chest.

This wasn't starting well. Hannah avoided looking at Niklas and motioned to the farmhouses scattered in the distance. "Your neighbors were some of the ones whose tools were stolen. By any chance, do you happen to know when it happened?"

She set her chin stubbornly. "No."

Undaunted, Hannah pressed on. "What about the tools? Do you know what was taken?"

"No."

"Edith."

She shrugged. "Just tools."

Niklas touched her elbow. "Hannah, we should go."

Hannah took a deep breath. "All right, Edith, I have a couple more questions for you, and I'm asking, as your friend, that you at least think a moment before you answer."

Edith shot a dour look at Niklas. "Fine. As your friend."

It wasn't much, but given Edith's mood, Hannah would take anything she could get. "Do you remember seeing anyone around the farms yesterday? Any visitors that you can remember?"

Edith started to shake her head and then stopped. "Well, Harmon rode by, but that's not unusual. He's good friends with most of the farmers around here."

Hannah's heart rate quickened. "Anyone else?"

"I think your uncle delivered a rocking chair. Other than that, I don't remember seeing anyone." She lifted her chin.

Obviously, she thought nothing of the information, but for Hannah, it was a ray of hope.

"One last thing." Seeing the stubborn frown that formed on Edith's face, she added, "Please? It'll only take a second."

At Edith's nod, Hannah forged ahead. "Do you remember when you told me that John Taylor was talking to Pa and Uncle Titus about Karl Mueller's land?"

Edith's gaze skipped to Niklas and back. "Yeah?"

"What exactly did they say, Edith? Did John say what he wants to do with the land?"

For the first time since they'd arrived, Edith looked uncomfortable. "Well, everyone knows he's been buying up land as fast as he can get his hands on it."

"So you think he's just trying to expand his holdings?" Niklas asked, before Hannah could respond.

Edith's face resumed its shuttered look. "I think he's wealthy and a businessman. He wants what they all want." She glanced at Hannah. "Anything else?"

"No. Thank you, Edith."

Her friend gave a grudging nod then motioned to the front of the house. "You two go on. Better if Pa doesn't see me talking with you."

She was right, of course. Hannah squeezed her arm before walking with Niklas toward the horses. After a moment, she stopped and strode quickly back to wrap Edith in a hug.

"Just give him a chance, would you? Before you believe anything you hear, give him the benefit of the doubt."

When she pulled away, Edith's face had softened from its harsh frown into something akin to a pained grimace. "Oh, Hannah. You like him, don't you?"

It wasn't a question that required an answer. Hannah gave her arm one last squeeze before joining Niklas.

"Well?" he asked as they mounted. "That's it then. It was Harmon who took the tools. Will you go home while I let the sheriff in Brookville know?"

"Not so fast, Niklas. You heard Edith. It's not unusual for Harmon to visit."

He shook his head as they urged the horses into a trot. "Not this time. This time, it's too much of a coincidence."

He was bunched tighter than a ball of twine. Hannah sensed it, as did his horse, who pranced skittishly and tossed his head against the tight hold Niklas kept on the reins.

"I agree that it would probably help your father for the sheriff to know that there were other people with opportunity to take the tools," she began. She held up her hand when he moved to speak. "But that's not what we're trying to prove, Niklas. The tools were in your cellar. We need to find out who put them there and why."

After a long moment, he agreed, but he didn't look happy about it. "All right then, what do you suggest? We go and talk to Harmon?"

"I hardly think that would prove helpful. If he did put the tools in your cellar, he's not about to admit it." She let go of the reins with one hand to pinch her lip. "No, I think Sally Bradshaw should be our next stop. She's been doing a lot of the talking, though Edith insists she's only repeating what she's heard. Maybe we should find out who she's hearing it from?"

He poked his hat back off his forehead, and to her surprise, he smiled. "You're good at this. If I haven't thanked you before now, I'm grateful you came along."

Her heart swelled at his praise, and at his smile...

She directed her gaze to the road ahead. Better if she didn't think about such things, at least for now.

So far as she knew, the Bradshaws were not ones who'd suffered any stolen tools, but when she thought about it, it could just have been because their farm was so far outside of town. By the time they reached their gate, Hannah was more than a little saddle sore and wishing she'd stopped to eat breakfast before heading out.

Before they'd even come to a stop, Ernest strolled out from behind the barn, his face slick with sweat and coated with soot. At his side walked his brother, Logan, by far the quieter of the two, but taller than Ernest by almost a head, and twice as thick. Soot smudged his face too, and Hannah wondered if they'd been burning something, a thought that was quickly chased away when Ernest nudged Logan and shot her a leering grin. Easing her mount closer to Niklas, she straightened her shoulders and lifted her chin.

Ernest shot Niklas a glower. "What are you two doing here?"

"We were hoping to see Sally," Hannah replied, nodding toward the house. "Is she home?"

Ernest spit a stalk of straw from his mouth and shook his head. "She's in town with Ma. Won't be home for a while. Besides"—his gaze shifted to Niklas, and Logan's followed—"she ain't likely to want to talk to a traitor."

Sensing Niklas tense, Hannah knew she had to act quickly. She leaned forward in the saddle. "Speaking of town, shouldn't you be at the store?"

Ernest turned back to her. "I decided that job wasn't for me."

He decided, or Mr. Smith did? Having been the victim of Ernest's shoddy work, she had no doubt it was the latter. And judging by the broken fence they'd passed and the barn door hanging haphazardly from a broken hinge, the pair were no better at home.

"We should go, Hannah," Niklas urged quietly.

"Yeah, you should go. I hear things are gonna be pretty busy at your place with your pa out of the picture," Ernest said.

"Maybe he'll be too busy to go around stealin'," Logan added, bunching his hand into a fist and pounding it into the palm of his other hand.

"That's ridiculous." Hannah snorted. "Anyone who knows the Muellers would never be foolish enough to repeat such nonsense."

"Careful, girl. You ain't so high and mighty. Before you go talkin' all big, maybe you ought to check with your family." Ernest nodded toward the gate. "Now, we'd appreciate it if you got off our land…you know, before anything bad happens."

The threat was clear. Hannah wheeled her horse around and headed for the gate. Niklas was slower to follow, and by the time they reached the road, she knew why. He was seething.

"Niklas—"

"I wish I had made that visit alone," he ground through clenched teeth. With the reins fisted in both hands, his knuckles shone white. "I'd have taught those fools a lesson."

"Then I'm glad you weren't alone," she replied. "The last thing you need is to be adding fuel to the rumors going around."

He shook his head stubbornly. "Not fuel. If anything, I'd make people think twice before they join in any gossip." He slapped the reins over his thigh, startling his horse. It took him a moment to get the animal back under control. "That was a wasted visit, and it cost us over an hour."

"It wasn't wasted," Hannah replied glumly, staring at the road ahead.

"What are you talking about? Sally wasn't even there."

"Not wasted." She flicked a glance at him, embarrassment making her face hot. "We know who's been starting the gossip. At least, some of it."

Niklas looked confused for a moment, and then his brow cleared. Obviously, he'd been so angered by Ernest's words it hadn't even registered what he'd said until now. The person responsible for the rumors, who'd fanned the talk turning people against the Muellers…was her pa.

## Chapter Twelve

Niklas reached for Hannah's hand then reined both horses to a stop. "Hold on there. I know what you're thinking, and I don't believe it."

Tears blurred her eyes as she shook her head. "Why not? You heard what Ernest said. He said I should check with my family."

"Your uncle Titus is family, isn't he? Maybe Ernest meant him."

Momentary relief flooded over her but was quickly dispelled when she remembered what her father had said about being at war with the Muellers.

Niklas leaned close to cup her cheek. "Come. Let's talk for a minute." He motioned toward a stand of trees then climbed from his horse and circled around to help her from the saddle. With her hand clasped tightly in his, he led her to a shaded spot, brushed away some twigs and grass, then pulled her down to sit.

"What is it you are thinking?" he asked, peering into her face intently. "I can see something is bothering you."

Hard as it was to admit, Hannah told him about her conversation with her father and the anger he'd displayed at her defense of them. Niklas listened silently, and when she finished, he drew up one leg, braced his elbow on it, and let out a heavy sigh.

"Your father believes we stole those tools, Hannah, and he believes we did it to keep proceeds from the crops from getting to his son overseas. I can see how that would anger him."

The fact that he was willing to give her father the benefit of the doubt when it wasn't reciprocated filled her with frustration instead of relief. "I don't understand. How can you be so gracious when—"

She wrested a handful of grass from the ground and threw it aside, wishing she could remove the fear and doubt plaguing her heart as easily.

"When you care for someone, you love who they love. And if that means overlooking an offense, then you do what must be done."

It took almost a full second for his meaning to break through her clouded thoughts. Her mouth fell open and she stared up at him, too stunned to speak.

Slowly, Niklas lifted his hand to run his thumb over her bottom lip. "I've always loved you, Hannah. I knew it years ago, when we were in school together, but now, seeing how you've defended me and my father and the lengths you'll go to help us, it only makes me love you more."

Hannah's heart beat harder the longer the moment stretched. Just when she thought he might kiss her, his hand fell.

"I wanted to tell you that before things change between us."

She blinked, trying to process his meaning. He stood and brushed the grass from his pants then reached for her hand.

"Niklas, wait."

He glanced up at the clouds gathering overhead. "I don't like the way that sky looks. We should get going." He kept his hand extended. Finally, she took it. Though there were a thousand things she wanted to say, the rest of the ride home was quiet.

When they reached the barn, Hannah watched as Niklas unsaddled her horse and led it to a stall.

"What will we do now?" she asked as he shut the stall door and slid the lock into place.

"I will search the cellar, see if there are any clues that were overlooked. Then I'll ride to Brookville to check on Papa."

He didn't meet her eyes when he said it, and she knew it was because he didn't want to tell her no when she asked if she could help. Her heart fluttered inside her chest. He'd told her that he loved her. Could she really let him go without telling him she loved him back?

She stepped toward him, palms sweating. "Niklas, before you go, there's something I'd like to tell—"

"What is this? What's going on here?" Pa stood outlined in the doorway, Harmon McDow at his shoulder. Lifting his finger to point at Niklas, he said, "You—get away from my daughter."

"Pa, it's not what you think."

"What I think is that every time I turn around, this man is finding a way to be alone with you."

"No, that's not—" Except, it kind of was. She swallowed and started again. "All right, we have been alone, but only to talk about what's been happening around town."

"Hannah, I want you to go inside. Now." He didn't wait for her response but stalked across the barn to clasp her elbow. "You're coming with me, young lady. And you." He shot a glare at Niklas. "Stay right where you are. I'll deal with you in a moment."

"You go on, William." Harmon stepped forward and gave a nod to Niklas. "I'll take care of him."

Hannah's heart slammed against her ribs. "What do you mean by that? He hasn't done anything wrong." Pulling against her father's hold, she threw a desperate glance at Niklas. "Tell them."

He met her gaze steadily, offering comfort instead of the fear he should be feeling. "Do as your father tells you, Hannah."

Stunned, she gave in to Pa's tug on her elbow. This made no sense. Any of it. How had things spiraled so out of control?

All the way to the house, Pa's stride grew longer, until Hannah nearly had to run to keep up. When they reached the house, he threw open the door then whirled to slam it closed. "How could you be so foolish? Having him here, after all they've done?"

"What have they done, Pa? They've been accused of stealing, but there's no proof it was them." The look in his eyes should have been warning enough. It wasn't. "You and Uncle Titus... You're the ones who've been spreading the rumors about them, aren't you? And the tools? It was Uncle Titus who suggested checking their house."

Pa tossed his head back in disgust.

"I heard him do it!" Hannah insisted. "And why? Why was that the first place he wanted to search?"

Though she nearly shouted, it was obvious Pa had stopped paying attention. He walked toward her, but instead of looking at her, he was focused on something outside the window. She followed the direction of his gaze, her blood running cold at what she saw.

"Is that...?"

"Smoke," he finished for her, his voice a choked whisper. "Get some water buckets, Hannah. The wheat field is on fire."

# Chapter Thirteen

*The wheat field is on fire.*

The words pounded through Hannah's brain and still she could make no sense of them.

"Hannah!"

Her father's shout snapped her from her trance.

"Go! Now!"

Hannah sped to the back of the house where they kept the rain barrels. They were large and bulky, but if she could keep them full with water from the well, maybe they could save some of the wheat.

The lack of rain had nearly emptied the barrels, but maybe that was a good thing. They'd be too heavy to lift full. Changing direction, Hannah raced back into the house, grabbing blankets and anything else that could be used to beat out flames. Plunging them into a trough, she soaked them through and was pulling them out when Pa and Harmon raced around the side of the house with the wagon.

"Where are those buckets?" Pa roared.

Hannah tossed him the sopping blankets. "Take these."

She ran back to the barrels, straining to drag the half-full one to the wagon. Instantly, Harmon leaped to the ground to help. As they worked, Niklas raced past for the second barrel and hauled it single-handedly into the wagon next to the first.

"Water, Hannah," he yelled.

Stumbling over her skirts, she ran to the well and let down the water bucket. Before it was fully up, Niklas was beside her with another bucket. Yanking the rope from her hands, he grabbed the full bucket and ran with it to the wagon while Hannah filled the second bucket. Harmon and Pa joined the line. Between the four of them, they had the rain barrels filled in record time.

Vaulting into the wagon, Pa slapped the reins, jolting the horses into motion almost before Harmon could throw himself into the back. They galloped off. A second later, Niklas followed, his horse's hooves kicking up clods of dirt and grass.

Though her arms and shoulders burned, Hannah refilled all four buckets. She left three sitting next to the well and took off with the fourth on foot. By the time she'd made it halfway across the field, her skirt was soaked and her hands ached. Still, she pushed on, coughing as the heat and smoke from the burning wheat grew thicker.

"Hannah, over here!"

Edith? Hannah squinted through the smoke to where Edith waved then set the bucket down and veered toward her.

"We saw the smoke." Edith shoved a spade into her hands and pointed. "We need to dig a trench here. Pa is working from the other side."

"But the water—"

She shook her head. "Your Pa and the others are trying to slow the fire, but it's spreading too fast. All we can do is try to save some of the field."

She pivoted and started digging. Hannah followed suit, shoveling until her hands were raw. Working until her eyes stung and the heat made her skirts steam. The smoke was so thick, she couldn't see more than a few feet ahead—not enough to know if they were working in a straight line or how far they had to go before they met Edith's father. If they met. In this haze, they could have worked right past each other and never known.

"There he is!" Edith yelled, then immediately started coughing.

Her hope revived, Hannah started digging faster, jamming the spade into the hardened ground and turning the soil as quickly as her aching arms would allow.

"We need more water!" a voice called through the smoke.

"They sound close," Edith choked out.

Scrubbing tears from her burning eyes, Hannah redoubled her efforts, grunting with each bone-jarring thrust of the spade. When, at last, their trench joined with Mr. Davis's, she turned back the way she came, widening the strip between their wheat and the encroaching flames.

Through the orange haze, more figures appeared—Henry Anderson, Uncle Titus, Pastor Beech, and others—all drawn by the smoke, same as the Davises. Hannah nearly sagged with relief at the sight of them, except she knew that somewhere out there, Niklas also fought the flames. Why couldn't she see him?

The wagon rumbled past, once, twice, three times? Hannah lost count as exhaustion crept through her limbs. Gradually, the shouts faded and a cool breeze blew away the smoke.

"Hannah. Hannah!"

Hannah looked to where Edith pointed. Though the ground still smoldered, orange flames no longer painted the gray sky.

Edith let her arms fall, the spade she clutched dropping from her fingers. "I think it's out."

"It's out?" Fresh tears soaked Hannah's eyes, only this time, they weren't caused by smoke. "It's out."

The moment she spoke the words, her legs began to tremble. She stumbled to Edith, and the two of them fell into each other's arms.

"How much…how much did we lose?" Looking around to gather her bearings, Hannah realized they weren't nearly as far from the house as she'd hoped. That meant they'd lost almost half the field. Her stomach sank.

"I need to find Pa." She started to pull away, but Edith's grasp on her hand stopped her.

"I'll come with you."

Grateful for her support, Hannah nodded then pointed to Edith's clothes. "Have a care with your skirt."

Here and there, small fires still burned, and Hannah had heard too many stories of a woman's petticoats being set ablaze.

Edith hiked her skirts high and followed as Hannah picked her way across the scorched field, each step an agony because she knew what the lost wheat would mean. With only half a crop to bring in, would they lose the farm? Would they even have enough seed to plant again next year?

A few yards away, a circle of soot-covered men gathered, sweat trails streaking their faces. Among them were Pa and Uncle Titus, both of them looking as fatigued and despondent as she felt.

"What started it, William?" Henry Anderson asked. "Any idea?"

Pa gestured to the overcast sky. "Had to be lightning, I guess. Nothing else I can figure."

Uncle Titus took a hankie from his back pocket and rubbed it over his face, smearing the soot even further. "Not lightning,

William. I'm sorry to be the bearer of more bad news but..." He stepped forward and pulled another square of fabric from his pocket. "I found this on the ground over there." He motioned across the blackened field. "Figure this is what caused the blaze. It's lucky I spotted it when I did or we might never have known what happened. I snatched it right before it went up in flames."

Hannah froze where she stood, dread crawling from her belly into her throat. The thing fluttering in Uncle Titus's hand was a rag no bigger than a handkerchief and charred on one end. Even so, she recognized it. She'd seen something similar in the Muellers' shop. It was one of the rags they used to polish the clocks.

# Chapter Fourteen

"What is that, Titus?" Pa strode toward him and snatched the rag from his hand. When he looked up, his eyes blazed from his blackened, sweat-stained face. "Where did you get this?"

"I told you, it was on the ground." Uncle Titus gazed around at the circle of silent men. "We all know what this means, don't we?"

"Titus." Pa's voice held a strange note of anger and pleading.

"Well?" Uncle Titus demanded, ignoring him.

Harmon McDow stepped forward to move alongside him. Shoulder to shoulder with Uncle Titus, they were a formidable pair. "This fire was no accident. Someone set it on purpose, and I think I know who."

"Hold on," Pastor Beech said, raising his hand. "Karl Mueller is in jail. There's no way he—"

"Not Karl, his boy," Harmon yelled, raising a fist over his head. "They're both in this together, trying to destroy our crops. And we know why, don't we!"

"No!" The yell ripped from Hannah's throat before she could stop it. She strode to her pa, uncaring that everyone stared. Or that her swishing skirt stirred embers. "Niklas was here when the fire started. There's no way he could have set it."

"Don't be ridiculous, girl," Uncle Titus growled, stepping toward her. "There's all kinds of ways to start a fire slow. A long fuse, even dampened cloth would do the trick." He shrugged and looked at Pa. "Well? What are we going to do about it?"

"I saw that boy a few moments ago." Harmon scowled as he lifted his hand to his eyes. "He was on the far side of the field. Likely he's still trying to set the rest of this crop on fire. I say we go and find him."

"He wouldn't do that!" Hannah spun, staring at the circle of faces, searching for a friendly one. She found it in Pastor Beech. "Please, you can't let them do this. Niklas is innocent."

"Hannah, you know I want to believe you—"

"You see?" Uncle Titus sneered. "Even the preacher knows what that boy did. Likely, he was angry that we locked up his pa and thought he'd get even."

Grumbling started from a couple of the men. Hannah knew she had to do something fast. She lifted her hands in appeal. "Of course he's angry. Anyone in his position would be. His father didn't take those tools."

"So, in your eyes, they're both innocent, is that it?" one of the men called.

She was losing this fight and had no idea what to do about it. She strode across the grass to Mr. Davis and Edith. "How many times has Karl Mueller helped your family? More than once?"

Next to the Davises stood Clarence Biggs. "How about you, Mr. Biggs?" Her gaze swung to John Taylor, who didn't look quite as grime-coated as the others. "Even you, with your plans to take the Muellers' land…how many times have they helped you?"

She walked in a slow circle, looking each man in the eye as she went. "The fact of the matter is that no one here has done more for this community than the Muellers have. They've been good neighbors to every single person here, and this is how we repay them?"

She stalked to her pa. If anyone would listen, it had to be him. "Pa, I know how bad this looks—the tools, this fire—but you have to believe me when I tell you I know it couldn't have been Niklas."

He hesitated a long moment then glanced at Uncle Titus, who shook his head. Slowly, he dragged his gaze back to her. "I'm sorry, Hannah. You've had your say, but now it's time we took matters into our own hands."

"William, please, just listen to her," Pastor Beech pleaded, struggling to be heard above a growing rumble among the men.

"Hannah, if there's something more you need to say, you'd best say it," Henry urged, his voice low.

At his words, the grumbling stopped and all eyes swung to her. But it was her pa's gaze that weighed the heaviest. He would be angry, no doubt, but that didn't matter. What mattered was clearing Niklas's name.

"I'm sorry, Pa," she said. She turned to face Uncle Titus and the rest of the men. "Niklas Mueller didn't set this fire. I know it for a fact because he was with me all day."

She felt everyone look from her to Pa. Suddenly, Hannah wished with all her might that the ground would open up and swallow her whole, so pained was the expression she saw on his face when she turned to him.

Surely, anger would have been better than the disappointment that seared her soul. Even then, she might have been able to face him. But to see him turn his back to her...

"Pa..."

"Hannah!"

Niklas? Hannah spun and spotted him. Like the other men, he was covered in soot from head to toe, his eyes wide. He started toward her.

She put up her hands to stop him. "Niklas, wait. Don't come over here."

She walked a couple of steps toward him. He broke into a run.

"Stop moving! Get on the ground, Hannah!"

He gestured wildly at her feet. As though in a dream, she looked down, confused by what she saw. More fire? And then realization hit, loosing a scream of panic that ripped from her throat.

Her dress was on fire.

## Chapter Fifteen

Hannah didn't have time to move. To think. When Niklas hit her, the force drove them both to the ground. For a second, she lay flat on her back, her lungs screaming for air that refused to come.

"Hannah!" Edith's scream pierced through her daze. A second later, her father's voice echoed Edith's.

"Hannah!"

She tried to sit up.

"Lie still!" Niklas shoved her back down, his hands beating at her legs, her feet.

She was on fire! Another scream broke through the dam that clogged her throat. "Put it out." She kicked her legs, trying desperately to get away from the flames. "Put it out!"

Fear made her blind. Deaf. She flailed her hands. Her feet. And then...Niklas's face was inches from hers, his hands gripping her arms.

"It's out, Hannah."

His voice came slowly into focus, like the volume on the radio Pa tinkered with gradually being turned up.

"The fire's out. You're all right."

She was all right? She looked down at her skirt. It was charred, but she felt no pain. No sickening burn. She *was* all right. A gasp heaved from her chest, followed by another. And another. And then Niklas was gathering her in his arms and helping her to stand.

"H-Hannah?" Pa's voice warbled from his throat, and then he ran to grab her in his arms. "Thank God you're all right. Thank You, God! I'm so sorry, Hannah. So sorry."

The last words groaned out of him, his voice as broken and agonized as the day they'd buried her mother.

Tears started down her face and that, coupled with Pa's crushing hold, made it hard to breathe. She lifted her head and craned her neck to peer up at him. "I'm sorry too, Pa."

"I, uh, I'm glad you're all right, Hannah." Uncle Titus neared to pat her on the back. "I didn't see that hot patch or I'd have warned you."

"I know, Uncle Titus." A few feet away, Henry stomped out the smoldering wheat stubble that had set her skirts on fire.

Uncle Titus sniffed, he too rubbing dampness from his eyes. "All right then, it's probably best if you womenfolk head on back to the house. We'll stay here and…finish up."

He cast a meaningful glance at Pa. She pulled free of her father's embrace. What did Uncle Titus mean by finishing up? She looked around for Niklas. Instead of congratulating him on his quick action, Harmon stood at his side holding one of his arms, Logan and Ernest Bradshaw on the other. Niklas's chest rose and fell, his breathing hard and his face set in stone.

Fear clutched her heart again, and she whirled to her father. "Pa?"

He met her gaze steadily then looked over at Uncle Titus. "Let him go, Harmon. You heard my daughter. There's no way he could've set that fire."

"But a fuse—" Uncle Titus began.

"Let it go, Titus." The authority in Pa's voice was undeniable, as was the look in his eyes. Crossing to Niklas, Pa put out his hand. "I know it wasn't you. Thank you for saving my daughter."

Harmon and Logan had no choice but to release Niklas. In that moment, Hannah knew without a doubt that, if they hadn't, and had the showdown flared into fisticuffs, whose side Pa would have been on.

Shaking out of their clasp, Niklas hesitated a moment and then shook Pa's hand, a grimace flashing on his face for a fraction of a second and disappearing. Flicking one last glance at Hannah, Niklas turned on his heel and strode off, not sparing a look at anyone else gathered around.

"Hannah, sweetheart, you should head to the house and check for burns." Pa's hand on her back was warm and comforting.

Still watching Niklas, Hannah shook her head. "I'm not burned, thanks to him."

"Regardless, you need to get out of that dress. Please, Daughter."

The word *daughter* pulled her attention away from Niklas. Worry added to the lines of fatigue that crisscrossed Pa's face, worry she could lessen if she obeyed. Besides, what was left to do here? At her side, Edith neared and looped her arm through Hannah's.

"I'll walk with you."

Hannah let Edith pull her toward the house. Neither said a word on the way, though Edith did make occasional clucking sounds accompanied by heavy sighs. Only after they reached the house and Hannah had washed and changed into a fresh dress, did Edith speak up.

"I'm so glad you're all right." She circled the kitchen table to wrap Hannah in a hug then pulled out a chair and patted the seat. "Sit. I made tea. I'll get you some."

Too tired to argue, Hannah took the chair she offered. "Thank you."

Edith nodded. Hannah looked around the kitchen. Not only had Edith made tea, she'd been busy slicing bread for sandwiches and fetching water for the men when they arrived. Now, she took a ham from the icebox and began cutting slender slices onto a plate.

"I can help." Hannah moved to rise.

"Uh-uh. Stay there." Edith grabbed the bread and carried it to the table along with a bowl of fresh butter. "You get the bread ready, and I'll finish the ham."

Once again, submitting took less effort than arguing. Hannah reached for the butter knife, muttering to herself when it slipped from her tired fingers and clattered onto the table, adding another ding to the diamond pattern.

For a long moment, Hannah simply stared.

Edith peered at her over her shoulder. "What is it? What are you looking at?"

"This." Hannah ran her finger over the table's edge. "We've had this table so long, I barely notice it anymore."

"What? The dents?" Edith set her knife down and crossed to join Hannah.

"No, the diamonds. See?" Hannah pushed aside the bread so Edith could see them.

"Huh." Edith shrugged then looked at Hannah curiously. "Goodness, Hannah, your family has had this table since before you were born. What's so fascinating about it now?"

"I've seen this pattern before," Hannah explained. She pushed back her chair, dropped to the floor, and scooted under the table, but the gathering gloom made it too dark to see. She poked her head out and peeked up at Edith. "Will you fetch me a lamp?"

Edith complied then joined Hannah under the table. "What are we looking for?" she asked, then grimaced when she smacked her head.

"A maker's mark." She turned the lamp wick higher and scoured the underside edge of the table.

"A what?" Edith rubbed her head. "What's a maker's mark?"

"A symbol stamped into furniture by the maker," Hannah said, exclaiming when a ripple in the wood caught her eye. Scuffling closer, she held the lamp high. "Here it is."

Crawling on her hands and knees, Edith edged closer to look. "All right, so your dad made this?" She eased out from under the table and grabbed a table leg. "He did a good job."

"Not Pa," Hannah said, handing her the lamp then following her out. "Uncle Titus. And you remember when I said I'd seen the pattern before?"

"Yeah." Edith stuck out her hand to help Hannah to her feet.

Brushing the dust from her hands, Hannah straightened. "It was at Niklas Mueller's house, Edith. What would they be doing with one of Uncle Titus's pieces?"

"Well…" Edith paused then started again. "It's a popular pattern. Maybe it's not one of his?"

She had a point. Hannah thought a moment. "You're right. I'll need to see their table again, check to see if it has Uncle Titus's mark. But if it does, why would they have it?"

Edith shrugged. "Maybe they bought it from him? He is a furniture maker, after all."

Hannah pinched her lip. "Hmm. Could be. But Pa said our two families have a history. Do you think maybe that table could be tied to whatever happened?"

Edith thought a moment, then she shook her head doubtfully. "I don't see how it could."

That wasn't the answer Hannah had been hoping for. She frowned as she went back to work buttering the bread for the sandwiches. Pa had definitely softened toward Niklas. His defense of him proved that. But was it enough for him to finally tell her what had happened between their two families to cause such animosity?

And if he wouldn't, who would?

# Chapter Sixteen

Friday morning dawned bright and clear. Except for the hint of smoke still lingering on the air, Hannah was tempted to think everything was right with the world. She emptied the last bit of corn from her bucket onto the ground for the chickens then went to refresh the water troughs.

Things weren't right, and no amount of wishful thinking would make it so. They still didn't know who'd set the fire. Silas still lay in a hospital somewhere across an ocean. Karl still sat in a jail cell awaiting his trial. And Niklas...

Hannah's heart sank as she remembered the look on his face as he'd walked away yesterday. Struck with a sudden thought, she hurried through the rest of her chores then went inside to wash up and change out of her work dress. The table was a perfect excuse to check on him, and since Pa was busy gauging the damage from the fire, now was her opportunity. For a split second, doubts about how her father would react when he learned she'd gone to see Niklas again plagued her thoughts. She pushed them away and hurried to the barn to saddle her horse.

Hannah was surprised to find that Niklas wasn't in the shop when she arrived. After securing her horse to a post, she walked up to the house and knocked on the door. Niklas answered almost immediately.

"Hannah. What are you doing here?"

His hair was washed and combed, but there was an ugly bruise on his cheek that she hadn't noticed the day before, and his shirt was only half-buttoned. It took her just a second to understand why.

"Your hands." Both were wrapped in gauze, the tips of his fingers on his right hand red and swollen where the bandages ended. She dragged her gaze up to look at him. "You burned yourself?"

"It's nothing." He leaned his shoulder against the door, one hand braced above his head. "You shouldn't be here. Do you want your father and uncle to be mad at you all over again?"

How would he get any work done with both hands injured? Hannah clamped her lips shut and pushed past him toward the kitchen. "Come inside. I'll help you clean those wounds."

Niklas refused to budge from the door. "You can't be here, Hannah. Not when it's just the two of us. It wouldn't be proper."

She spun and jammed both hands onto her hips. "Right now, that's the least of my worries. Of course, the longer you stand there arguing with me, the longer this whole process takes." She pointed to the kitchen. "Well?"

"Fine," he growled after a moment, "but we're leaving the door open." He nudged it wider with his foot then followed her down the hall. "How is your father's field? Does he know how much he'll be able to save?"

She lowered her gaze and busied herself collecting water and a soft cloth to use on his hands. "Not yet. He was out looking when I left." She pulled a chair forward and gestured him into it then carried the water and towels to the table before taking out a second chair and seating herself. She patted the tabletop. "Put your hands up here."

He rested his arms on the table, palms up. Carefully, she peeled back the layers of gauze. At the sight of the blisters that covered one of his hands, Hannah stifled a gasp. Thankfully, the other hand was just red and slightly swollen in places.

"There's salve in the cupboard." He angled his head to a shelf next to the stove. "It helped some with the pain."

"And the gauze?"

"Next to the salve."

Hannah hurried to fetch both then set to work cleaning the old salve and traces of soot from his hands. Once fresh salve was applied, she rewrapped Niklas's hands, tucking the ends of the bandages into place instead of pinning so he would be able to easily remove them later.

"I'm glad I came," she said, patting the last little trailing piece of bandage into place.

"Me too."

She touched the bruise on his cheek, anger rifling through her midsection. She didn't have to guess where he'd gotten it.

He swallowed hard and slid his hands onto his lap. "You still haven't told me why you're here."

She blinked in surprise. She'd been so focused on Niklas, she'd forgotten all about the table.

"Oh." She jumped to her feet and rapped her knuckle on the table. "I came to look at this."

Motioning for him to get up, she pushed the chairs out of the way then tipped the table onto its side.

"Hannah, what in the world are you doing?"

"I'm looking for something."

She dropped to her knees and began examining the table's edge, down one side, along the other edge, and up the other side. Nothing.

Niklas squatted next to her. "Much as I enjoy your company, do you mind telling me what we're looking for?"

"A maker's mark. I was sure I'd find it."

She narrowed her eyes to peer into the crevice created where the table leg met the top. In all four corners, a brace fixed one side of the table to the other, adding stability and strength. Could it be?

Careful examination revealed nothing in the first corner, or the second. But the third...

"Here it is." Hannah pointed eagerly, and Niklas bent low to examine the spot.

"Is that an arrow?" he asked, squinting.

"It is. And if you look carefully, you can see a *TW* hidden in the wood grain. Uncle Titus's initials," she explained, gripping one of the legs. "My uncle built this table."

Niklas shook his head, his brow wrinkling in confusion. "But this was my mother's table. I always thought it was passed down to her from a relative."

"Did your father tell you that?"

Niklas's mouth worked, and then he shook his head again.

"All right." Hannah stood and righted the table with a little help from Niklas. "So, let's talk about the reasons why your family would have something my uncle made."

"They could have bought it," Niklas said, leaning against the back of a chair.

"Or it could have been a gift." Hannah raised her eyebrows. "A wedding present?" She frowned. "In either case—whether they bought it or it was a gift—it would have had to have been before whatever incident happened between them, don't you think?"

"That would make sense." Niklas started to scrub his fingers against his cheek, remembered the bandages, and let his hand fall to his side. "The only way to know for sure is to ask those involved, and my father isn't talking."

"Neither is mine." Hannah lifted both hands, palms up. "So? Who does that leave?"

"Your uncle Titus."

She nodded. After yesterday's events, she figured the last thing Niklas wanted was another run-in with her uncle, but if the fire wasn't tied to the history between their families, what else could it be? She bit her lip, thinking.

"Niklas, let's forget about Uncle Titus for a moment and focus on John Taylor. He was present after the fire started, but did you notice he wasn't nearly as covered in soot as anyone else? Is it possible he was the one who started the fire?"

Niklas frowned. "Why would he do that? I thought he and your father were friends."

"More like business acquaintances," Hannah said. "And it's a known fact he's been trying to get his hands on your father's land. Why wouldn't he do the same with ours?"

Folding his arms over his chest, Niklas shrugged. "It's likely, I suppose, but he didn't set the fire. I saw him and his wife pull up in that fancy car of theirs. They even had their daughter with them.

Besides, I can't believe he'd dirty his hands like this. Even if he were the type, he'd hire it done."

She had to admit he was right.

"What about Harmon?" Niklas continued. "He hates my family, sure enough."

"But he was with Pa all morning." She shook her head. "It couldn't have been him."

Niklas grunted. "Then I suppose we're back where we started."

Apparently so. She grabbed the gauze and salve and returned both to the cupboard where she'd found them.

"All right, I'll ride out to Uncle Titus's place and let you know what he says," she said, closing the cupboard door.

"Hold on, I'm going with you." He caught her by the hand as she walked past, wincing at the contact.

"Niklas, your burns." She froze and stared at their joined hands, afraid to pull away lest she hurt him more.

"You've already tried to help me, Hannah. I can't let you do this alone."

"I've helped you?" She sighed and stepped closer to run her fingers along his stubbled cheek. "You saved my life. Your hands are burned because of it. I'd say I still owe you."

"You don't owe me anything."

She pulled away, afraid of the feelings the hoarseness in his voice stirred in her chest. Still, he clung to her hand. She had the feeling he would continue until she agreed to let him come. Slowly, she nodded. "First, tell me one thing." She pointed to his cheek. "Did Harmon give you that?"

His lips turned up in a wry grin, and he touched his knuckles to the bruise. "Still packs a pretty good punch for his age."

Hannah gave a snort of disgust. "How can you joke? He could have hurt you."

"No, he couldn't. The first punch caught me by surprise. I was ready for the second one." He eased slightly closer, cupping her neck in both hands. "And even if he had hit me again, it wouldn't have mattered. You were the only thing I could think about."

"Niklas…" She whispered his name, her eyes drifting closed.

He blew out a long sigh and let his hands fall. "We should go."

Except, she didn't want to leave. She wanted to be close to him forever, wanted this moment to last. But then reality intruded, and she snapped her eyes open. He was right. They still had to figure out who'd really set the fire, and more and more, she was beginning to suspect that whatever happened between their families had something to do with it.

Drawing in a shaky breath, she lifted her hand to smooth her hair then drew her shoulders back. Plenty of time to think about what was happening between her and Niklas later. Right now, she needed to focus on the task at hand, which was saddling up their horses.

Except focusing wasn't so easy, especially a few minutes later with him riding alongside her, so undeniably handsome, even with the bruise on his cheek and stubble lining his jaw. In fact, he looked even more rugged than normal.

He turned his head and caught her staring, and Hannah had to scramble to keep from dropping the reins.

"A-Almost there," she stammered, too embarrassed to look at him, even when he chuckled.

His low laugh faded as they drew closer to the house. Despite a number of eligible women in Panic, Uncle Titus had never married, and it showed in the austerity of his home. No curtains fluttered at the half-open windows, no flowers filled the boxes around the stairs.

Niklas inclined his head to the door. "Is he home?"

"I thought he would be."

They climbed from their horses, and Hannah handed her reins to Niklas and went to knock on the door. When her uncle didn't answer, she turned to Niklas and pointed to the barn.

"Maybe he's down there? That's where he works on his furniture. I'll go look."

"Want me to come along?"

She did, but she wouldn't risk him getting hurt again defending her. "No need. I'll be right back."

Inside, the barn was cool and dark, but the usual odor of wood chips and sawdust was missing, overpowered by something more acrid and oily. Kerosene?

Hannah frowned and pushed the door open wider. "Uncle Titus?"

Pigeons cooing from the rafters was the only response. Hannah moved farther into the barn, the oily smell growing with each step. Could he have knocked over a lamp? Or what if…

Her heart skipped a beat. What if whoever had set their field on fire was trying the same thing here?

She ran back to the door and gestured for Niklas. "Come quick!"

He lashed the reins to a hitching post and came running. "What is it?"

"Do you smell that?" Hannah made a circle in the air with her finger.

Niklas paused to sniff. "Kerosene."

"That's what I thought."

"Where is it coming from?"

"I don't know." She grasped his arm. "Niklas, what if someone is trying to burn down my uncle's shop?"

His jaw hardened. "Let's spread out. You start looking around here. I'll check the stalls. And Hannah…" He cupped her cheek. "If you see fire, get out."

She nodded, the fear in her belly growing as Niklas sprinted toward the far end of the barn. Hiking up her skirts, she crossed to the tack room and threw open the door. Nothing. In fact, the odor seemed less pungent here. She closed the door and kept moving. In the feed room, bags of corn and oats lay ripped open, spilling contents onto the wood floor, but messes like this were not uncommon for Uncle Titus. Hannah shut the door.

"Anything?" Niklas's shout echoed through the barn, disturbing the restless pigeons and sending them fluttering for safety.

"No. You?"

"No." A stall door creaked on rusted hinges as Niklas swung it closed. "Keep looking."

Hannah hurried her steps, checking through stalls until she met Niklas in the middle. "I don't understand," she said, walking in a tight circle. "The smell seems like it's coming from right here."

Niklas tipped his head back and looked up. Hannah followed suit. The hatch above them was open, and she could see the dark hole through which Uncle Titus threw hay from the loft.

"I'll check," Niklas said, reaching for the string that pulled down the stairs.

He scrambled up and disappeared nimbly through the hole. Hannah stood watching as dust stirred by his boots filtered through the cracks in the floor. A short while later, his head appeared in the opening.

"Nothing. I can hardly even smell the kerosene up here."

Hannah motioned for him to come down. By now she'd almost grown accustomed to the smell and wondered if her nose was playing tricks on her.

"Wait a minute." Niklas kicked aside some of the straw on the floor with his toe. "What is that?"

"What? I don't see anything."

Niklas dropped to his knees and, using his good hand, scraped aside more of the straw from the floor. Underneath was a board that looked as though it had been pried up and then hastily replaced. But what caught Hannah's eye was a bit of white poking up from a slender crack.

"Let me." After dropping to her knees next to him, Hannah struggled to get her fingers under the board, to no avail. "Wait, I saw a file in the workroom."

She leaped to her feet and took off at a run and came back with the file. Using the pointed end, she jammed it under the board and managed to pry it up an inch. Niklas grabbed the edge and pulled it up the rest of the way. With the board gone, the odor of kerosene was unmistakable.

Pinching one corner of the cloth, Niklas held it up, his eyes widening in anger and disbelief. "This is one of the rags from our shop."

Hannah reached into the hole and found another cloth. "This one too."

Huffing a breath, Niklas shoved to his feet. "It was Titus. Titus set the field on fire, and he used this"—he held out the rag—"to make sure it looked like I'd done it."

Hannah dropped the rag as though it were a living thing. She wished with all her might it wasn't true, but what other explanation was there?

"We need to go. We need to show this to someone." Niklas shoved the cloth into his back pocket and reached for her hand. "C'mon, Hannah."

"Niklas, wait." She looked around helplessly. "There has to be—"

"What? An explanation? A reason?" He dropped his hand to glare at her. "The people in this town hate us, Hannah, and for no other reason than the fact that we're German. Your uncle?" He slashed his finger through the air. "He's just a symptom of what I sensed has been going on for a while."

Hannah shook her head slowly. "That's not true, Niklas. The people in this town have stood up for you. Henry and Pastor Beech—"

He held up two fingers. "Two people, Hannah, out of a whole town. You think I don't know what the rest are saying? Wondering why I'm here while everyone else has gone off to fight?"

He raked his burned hand through his hair, dislodging Hannah's carefully wrapped bandage. "It's because of my father, Hannah. That's why I didn't enlist. Because I'm all he has left and he begged me to stay. And I listened—even though I go to bed sick to my stomach, thinking about our friends and neighbors, over there dying while I'm here. Doing what?"

She had no answer.

His chest still heaved, but with her silence the rage seemed to go out of him. His shoulders slumped, and he turned his back to go.

"Niklas, wait."

But she needn't have bid him stay, because there, standing in the doorway, was Uncle Titus.

## Chapter Seventeen

"How dare you?" Raw anger thrummed through Uncle Titus's tone. Even his body seemed to vibrate. Stepping farther into the barn, he glared, his hands clenched into fists at his sides. "What do you think you're doing in my barn?"

Hannah rushed forward to stand between her uncle and Niklas. "He's with me, Uncle Titus. I brought him. I wanted to talk to you."

He flicked her a cursory glance then refocused his attention on Niklas. "Your father is alone because he didn't care about anyone but himself. He wanted a son, and by God, he was going to do whatever it took to get one."

Shocked into silence, Hannah stared at him.

"What are you talking about?" Behind her, Niklas's voice was hard as steel.

"He never told you?" A grunt rumbled from Uncle Titus's chest. "Figures he'd be too cowardly to admit what he'd done."

Niklas strode forward. Hannah caught his arm.

"Are you calling my father a coward?" he growled through clenched teeth.

"No more than his son," Uncle Titus shot back.

"Uncle Titus, stop!" Hannah spun to push against Niklas's chest. "Don't listen to him."

"That's right, don't listen to me, boy. Don't listen to the truth about what happened to your mother."

Hannah opened her mouth, but the words that proceeded did not come from her.

"That's enough, Titus."

"Pa?" Her knees nearly gave out with relief at the sound of his voice. And he wasn't alone. Henry and Pastor Beech were with him. "Pa, Niklas didn't set the fire."

"I know that, Hannah."

"No, what I mean is"—she let go of Niklas to run to him—"we found something, Pa. We came to talk to Uncle Titus, but while we were here, I smelled kerosene. At first, I thought the same person who set fire to our wheat was trying to burn down his barn, but instead we found—"

"Rags doused in kerosene." He didn't sound surprised. Or even angry. "I know."

She backed up a step, trying to read on his face what her heart was already screaming. "How...did you know?"

He dropped his gaze. When he didn't answer, Hannah forced herself to ask again. "Pa, how did you know about the rags?"

The barn had gone silent. Even the pigeons no longer cooed. Slowly, Pa's head lifted. "I stole the rags from the Muellers' place. I'm the one who set the fuse and burned the wheat."

"No." Hannah held up her hand to stop anything else he might say. "That doesn't make any sense. Why would—?"

"Just listen to what he has to say, Hannah," Pastor Beech said, coming to stand beside her.

Eyes wide, Hannah turned to her father.

"The wheat looked bad, Hannah. No rain. No men to help with the harvest. I bought seed on credit after the government passed the Federal Farm Loan Act last year, but with no crop to bring in, I was afraid we'd lose everything. So I took out an insurance policy. I figured the money would at least give us something."

She could hear the words that came from his mouth but could make sense of none of them. "But you were with Harmon. There's no way either of you could have—"

"It's like Titus said. I set a long fuse."

He said Uncle Titus's name but wouldn't look at him. Suspicion sparked in Hannah's brain. "If that's true, why hide the evidence here? Why not get rid of the rags back home, or burn them?"

Pastor Beech and Henry both swiveled to Pa.

"Well, William?" Henry asked.

"I tried, but then Harmon came along, and I didn't have time."

"So, you hid them in the tack room," Hannah said.

"William—" Uncle Titus began.

"I had no choice," Pa cut in before he could finish. "I was trying to take care of my family."

Hannah shook her head, her eyes filling with tears. "Oh, Pa. You still are."

He looked at her then. "What do you mean?"

She turned to Uncle Titus. "Aren't you going to say something?"

"He's got nothing to say," Pa replied. Then he gestured to Pastor Beech and Henry. "I'd appreciate it if one of you could give me a ride into Brookville."

"No, William." Where moments ago Uncle Titus had sounded belligerent and angry, now he sounded defeated and weak. "I can't let you do this. Not again."

"Be quiet, Titus."

"Not this time." He stepped forward, past Hannah and Niklas, to his brother. Clapping his hand on his shoulder, he said, "You've always taken care of me, haven't you?"

"I always will," Pa replied. "Just don't say any more."

Uncle Titus laughed wryly. "I don't have to. You already have." He crossed to the loose board, kicked it free, and pulled out one of the rags. "They weren't in the tack room, William."

Pa's mouth worked. "Well…I…made a mistake."

"I'm the one always making mistakes. Ever since we were kids. But I never worried about it because I always had you to bail me out of trouble." Tears filled his eyes as he dropped the rag. "I won't let you do it this time, Brother." Drawing a deep breath, he looked at Pastor Beech and Henry. "I'm the one who set the fire and stole those tools. This here"—he gestured to the floor—"is proof."

"Why?" Niklas's voice startled them all. He walked toward Titus, chest heaving. "What have I ever done to make you hate me so much?"

Titus hunched his shoulders and shifted his weight to one leg. Slumped like that, Hannah could have felt sorry for him, if she hadn't been so angry.

"I didn't hate you, boy, I blamed you. It was your father I hated."

"Why?" Hannah repeated, going to stand next to Niklas. "What happened between you?"

Titus's mouth worked, but no words came out.

"It was Belinda." Pa too stepped forward. "He loved her from the day they met. For a while, we all thought she loved him too."

"I asked her to marry me," Titus said. "Gave her a table for a wedding present."

Hannah glanced up at Niklas. "The one in your kitchen."

Titus's eyes widened, and his gaze bounced from Hannah to Niklas. "She kept it?"

Instead of answering his question, Niklas asked, "If she loved you, how did she end up with my father?"

"I never said she loved me. Not like him," Titus replied. "It was over for me the moment she laid eyes on him. I begged her to reconsider, but she wouldn't listen. She married him. And when she died giving birth to you, I went a little mad." He stopped and looked at Pa. "I didn't mean to set your field on fire. It was just supposed to be a small blaze, something to catch people's attention. And then I was going to put it out and everyone would think I was a hero, especially when I showed up with that rag to prove it was deliberately set. But it grew so fast, and the wind… It all got away from me. I'm so sorry, William."

A groan cut from his throat, and he covered his face with his hands, sobbing.

Niklas stared at him for a long moment then backed away a step, shaking his head. "I…cannot…"

Hannah stretched out her hand to him, but he refused to take it.

"I'm sorry, Niklas," Pa said, moving to him. "I suspected what Titus had done with the tools. He knew exactly which part to take that would disable the binder. Your father wouldn't have known that. Still, I didn't want to believe it. And I suppose I was a little angry at you and your father too."

"Because of Silas?" Niklas whispered.

Pa looked at him, sheer misery twisting his features. "I knew your family wasn't to blame. But something inside me hated the war so much. Hated Germany so much. I just..."

He lifted his hands then let them drop to his sides. "I let my fear and hatred consume me. I'm sorry."

Niklas said nothing. Finally he walked past Henry and Pastor Beech and out of the barn.

"Pa?" Hannah grasped his arm and looked up at him pleadingly.

His lips curved in a sad, understanding smile. "Go," he whispered.

It was all the urging Hannah needed. Hiking her skirts, she ran out of the barn. Already, Niklas had his horse unhitched and was preparing to mount.

"Niklas, wait!" She ran toward him, stumbling once then dropping her skirts to run harder.

The reins fell from his fingers, and then he too was running, slowing down just enough to sweep her into his arms and claim her mouth in a kiss.

Slowly, achingly, he set her on her feet. Even so, he held her tight, his mouth pressed against her hair. "Your father?"

"He knows," she whispered, her tears soaking his shirt. "I'm so sorry, Niklas."

"It wasn't you," he soothed, one hand stroking her back.

"But you were right. You said people were saying things, feeling things, and I didn't want to believe you. I should have listened."

"No, Hannah." He pulled away just enough to look into her face. "I've been so angry I was only focused on the bad things that were happening. I should have been looking for the good—like you, and Henry, and Pastor Beech. Maybe if I'd had a little more faith, I would have trusted that things would work out."

He touched her cheek and then pressed another kiss to her lips. "But you never lost faith, did you?"

"That's not true. There were t-times I wasn't sure."

She stumbled over the words because admitting her weaknesses was hard. But somehow, knowing it was Niklas she said them to made it better, as though she knew her secrets were safe with him and always would be.

"I love you, Niklas. Yesterday—" Was it only yesterday? She shook her head. "You said you loved me, but then you left, and I was going to tell you I loved you too, but then the fire happened and, well, it all seems so long ago now."

The words spilled out, and with so much emotion building in her chest, she was helpless to stop them.

Niklas put his finger over her lips, silencing her. She stared at him, fresh tears burning her eyes.

"Hannah, you love me? Are you sure? Because I—" He stopped, tears filling his own eyes. "I love you so much. You're everything to me. You always have been, only I've never had the courage to say it before now."

Hannah rose onto her tiptoes and pressed a kiss to his mouth, smiling as he fell into a shocked silence of his own. "I'm sure, Niklas. I love you. I always have. And I always will."

Without a word, Niklas pulled her to his chest and held her there. Resting her cheek against his shirt, Hannah smiled. She didn't know what would become of Karl, or Uncle Titus, or any of them after this war. Certainly, there would be more changes to come, more battles to face here at home and overseas. There was no doubt things in Panic would never be the same. But she was all right with that now. She'd made her peace. Because come what may, she had everything she would ever need or want, right here in her arms.

# Chapter Eighteen

*May 1918*

The whistle of the incoming train beckoned people onto the Brookville train platform. Jostling with the rest of them, Hannah stretched onto her tiptoes, trying to see the railcar door above the hats and plumes that blocked her view.

"Anything?" Next to her, Karl also scanned the windows of the train as it groaned and squealed and rocked to a stop.

"Not yet." Cupping her hand over her eyes to shut out the glare of the sun, Hannah whispered a small prayer. "God, please?"

It had been almost a year since Niklas enlisted. A year since he'd put a slender silver ring on her finger moments before she'd waved him off to war on this very train.

But the war was over now and he was coming home. Her heart beat hard against her ribs.

"Well?" Pa sidled closer and clasped her elbow. "Do you see him?"

"No." A waver troubled her voice. She grasped her father's fingers tightly. "Pa, where is he?"

Pa looked at her and smiled. "Steady, Daughter. You'll be with your husband soon."

Her husband. She could hardly believe it. Letting go of his hand, Hannah managed to squeeze a couple of inches closer to the train.

*in Panic, Pennsylvania*

Up and down the platform, squeals of excitement and joy rang out as families reunited with their brothers, husbands, sons.

And then there was Niklas.

Everything else faded. He was leaner than when he'd left, his cheeks more gaunt and his eyes more hooded. But then he pulled a bag off his shoulder and opened his arms, and Hannah's heart fluttered as she ran into them.

"Niklas!"

She screamed his name, laughing in delight as he swept her up and kissed her soundly. Finally, he was home. Home! And they'd never have to spend another day apart again.

"Thank God, you're here," she managed, between kisses. "You're safe."

"I'm safe, thanks to your prayers," he replied. Setting her down reluctantly, he scanned the crowd. "Where's Papa?"

"Here." Karl raised his hand and waved then motioned to Hannah. "But I thought I'd let you greet your wife first."

Grinning, Niklas walked to his father and grasped his shoulder. "I'm home, Papa."

Tears streamed down Karl's face. "Yes, you are." Grabbing him by the lapels on his uniform, Karl yanked Niklas into a hard embrace. "My boy is home."

The words sparked sadness in Hannah's chest. Niklas was home, and Silas too, though pain from his injuries still troubled him when the weather was bad. But many boys from Panic weren't home and never would be. Surprisingly, the first name that leaped to mind was Ernest Bradshaw. He'd enlisted when he turned eighteen and had quickly become one of the first fighting casualties from their small town.

Uncle Titus was gone too, though not because of the war. After the truth came out about what he'd done, he sold his land to John Taylor and gave the money to Pa to pay off his seed loan. Last she'd heard, he was living somewhere in Brookville, working for a furniture maker so he didn't have to worry about keeping up with orders.

Pa eased to her side. "You all right? You seem lost in thought."

She shrugged and swiped a tear from her eyes. "So much has changed."

He bobbed his head in agreement. "Times change. They have to." He pulled her into a hug. "I'll go wait with the others."

Hannah nodded. He would greet Niklas eventually. Right now, she didn't doubt that he was still plagued by a little doubt and embarrassment. But now that Niklas was home, that would ease in time.

Niklas pulled away from his father's arms and picked up his bag then reached out his hand to Hannah. "Shall we go home?"

"Not yet." She glanced at Karl, who pointed to the station. "There's someone else here who wants to greet you."

"Your pa?" Niklas smiled down at her. "Did I tell you that he wrote to me? Several times, in fact." He shifted the pack on his shoulder. "I have them all right here. I'll show them to you later, if you want."

"I'd like that," she whispered. Slipping her arm around his waist, she leaned into her husband's side, walking with him stride for stride toward the small, wooden station.

At the door, Niklas reached around her to hold it open. Hannah hurried inside then took Karl's hand and stood with him facing Niklas.

*in Panic, Pennsylvania*

It was much quieter inside the station. With the exception of those outside their group, no one spoke. For several seconds, Niklas just stared, confusion wrinkling his brow.

Hannah smiled wider, her chest as near to bursting as it had ever been. Pastor Beech was here, alongside her pa and Henry Anderson, but so were Edith and the rest of the Davises, and Clarence Biggs. John Taylor was here with his family. The Flynns. Morrises. Christensons. The list went on and on. In fact, there weren't many from Panic who hadn't turned out in support of the Muellers on this special day.

Niklas slowly lifted his hand to point at a banner that read WELCOME HOME, NIKLAS!

"What...is this?" He lowered his gaze to meet Hannah's. "Did you do this?"

"Not me," Hannah replied, pressing her hand to her chest at the look she saw on her husband's face. "Pastor Beech did it."

"Not just me," he clarified quickly, stepping forward to shake Niklas's hand. "It was the town, Niklas. They all wanted to be here to welcome you home."

Hannah didn't think her heart could be any fuller, but then Pa approached, his shoulders hunched humbly. Neither man spoke for a moment, but then they were hugging. Who initiated the embrace Hannah couldn't tell, but it didn't matter now.

Clearing his throat, Niklas pulled away and faced the small crowd. "I want to thank you all for coming. This"—he raised his hand and let it fall helplessly—"means more than you'll ever know."

"Welcome home, Niklas!" The shout seemed to break the dam, and a flood of well wishes and welcome homes followed.

It was several minutes before Hannah could make her way to her husband again, but she didn't mind. He needed this, and she needed to see it.

Raising his hands, Karl called for the crowd's attention. "My son and his wife never had a wedding reception. I would like you all to join us back at our place." Winking at Hannah, he said, "It's been too long, but we will finally celebrate their marriage with them, yes?"

Another cheer went up, and Hannah couldn't help but smile.

"Well then? What are we waiting for?" Henry yelled. "Let's go!"

"Wait, wait!" Niklas waved one hand and searched the crowd for Hannah. Finding her, he wove his way to her. He grabbed her hand and dropped to one knee.

Hannah flushed with shy embarrassment. "What are you doing?"

Niklas's smile spread as he reached inside his uniform. "Isn't it obvious? I'm asking you to marry me."

"Niklas." Hannah tugged on his hand, but he refused to budge. She bent close to whisper, "We're already married."

A low ripple of laughter drifted from the crowd.

"Yes, but not properly. Not with our family and…our friends gathered around." He looked around at the sea of faces, fresh tears glistening in his eyes, and settled back on her. "This time, I'd like to do it right."

He took out a small box, pulled off the top, and held it up for her to see. Inside was nestled a shiny gold band, a small diamond glinting at its center. Hannah gasped in delight and pressed her hand to her mouth.

"Hannah Elizabeth Walker, will you marry me?"

Hannah was too choked to speak. Behind Niklas, her pa and Karl stood arm in arm, both smiling proudly, even wiping away tears of joy now and again. She looked down at her husband. Her confidant. Her best friend.

"Yes..." She swallowed hard and started again. "Yes, I'll marry you."

A cheer went up, but Hannah barely heard. Jumping to his feet, Niklas kissed her hard then slid the gold band onto her finger next to the silver one.

"I love you, Hannah Walker."

"I love you too," she said. She pulled back to smile at him. "But it's Mueller now."

He smiled and kissed her again.

It was Mueller. And it always would be.

# No Fear In Love

*by*
Barbara Early

God is too good to be unkind and He is too wise to be mistaken. And when we cannot trace His hand, we must trust His heart.

—Charles Haddon Spurgeon

## Chapter One

*Panic, Pennsylvania*
*Present Day*

Amy Frye tucked a stray lock of hair into her warm wool hat and took a mental inventory of the burgeoning contents of the dimly lit farmhouse kitchen. The counters were covered with boxes of wrapped baked goods. A dozen or so mismatched vacuum bottles stood ready and, if Amy knew her friend Winnie Franklin, were already filled with steaming coffee, sweet hot cocoa, and spiced warm cider. The very air around her was still hazy with flour and infused with the scents of cinnamon, cloves, nutmeg, and ginger.

Winnie exited the pantry with a box of cups and lids. "I appreciate your help, but are you sure you want to leave this early? Most people won't be wandering the park until the sun warms things up a bit. I don't even think the groundhog is awake. If you wait until the others are up…" She gestured to the rest of the house, where the residents of Chanan Home still slept. "You know they love to help."

The "they" to which Winnie referred were the five young-adult residents of the group home for the developmentally challenged that Winnie ran in the large, renovated farmhouse that Amy rented to them.

"I know," Amy said. "But I'd like to get us a good spot. It snowed last night, so I might need to shovel it out before setting up the tent."

"I can at least help carry things out," Winnie said, shrugging her coat on over her ample figure. Winnie was at least ten years older than Amy but had always been tight-lipped about her age. Her milk-chocolate complexion was, as always, accented with the perfect amount of makeup, although heavy glasses hid her eyes. She wore her hair cropped close to her head and always the same silver pendant around her neck.

"You know," Winnie said, "you are by far the best landlord I ever had. I don't know why you don't set up your own booth. I mean, your hand-dyed yarn is just beautiful. The tourists would gobble it up."

"Hand-dyed yarn isn't for everyone. They'd pick up a skein, ooh and aah over it, spot the price tag, and set it right back down."

"I thought you sold a bunch of it."

"Yes, but more online than in the shop. And most of that's to fashion students and dyed-in-the-wool knitters." Amy cringed at her unintentional but dreadful pun. "It's labor intensive, so it costs that much more. Most people don't appreciate the reason for the markup. Meanwhile, I enjoy helping." Amy picked up a box of muffins, pausing a moment to inhale the heavy scent of ginger. "And don't forget, that grant to teach your residents helps pay my bills too."

Several trips later, Amy climbed into her overloaded Civic, cranked the heater, and switched on the headlights. They'd crammed most of the baked goods into the back seat and trunk and bundled the hot drinks on the floor behind her. Winnie would bring the remainder later, along with the Chanan House residents, prior to the official start of the festivities. On the passenger seat next to her sat Amy's contribution to their fundraiser, a box containing dozens of little *amigurumi* groundhogs that she and the residents had crocheted in the yarn shop just across the parking lot in the old barn she'd converted into her shop and residence.

Winnie rushed back to the farmhouse, her breath like the smoke from a train engine illuminated in the car's headlights.

Amy removed her gloves, reached into the back seat, and wrestled a gingerbread muffin from a box. She took the first bite before she turned onto the road. The tender, spicy muffin melted on her tongue, tasting as marvelous as it smelled, especially paired with the unexpected lemon drizzle on top. She licked her fingers as she navigated the hills and curves, the rural roads bordered with the occasional farmhouse, barn, or roadside stands that would remain closed until the next harvest. When she reached the road sign that heralded she was leaving Panic, Pennsylvania, she put on her turn signal and headed the nine or so miles to Punxsutawney.

---

Guy Coraggio stifled a yawn just as he spied the first sign announcing his arrival in Punxsutawney, the "Weather Capital of the World," or so heralded the billboard with the giant, grinning groundhog. He glanced at the cloud cover. Snow clouds rolled east, but the sky was still milky white. If today was Groundhog Day, there probably wouldn't be a shadow. Not that he planned to stay that long.

He was trying to recall whether that meant six more weeks of winter or an early spring when he hit the first detour sign.

"Roads can't be closed already," he mumbled to himself. "The big event is still days away."

Guy followed the prescribed detour signs past a park filled with pop-up tents and people milling about. On the next block, a banner hanging over the street proclaimed the annual Groundhog Days celebration. *Days*, plural. They took their groundhog seriously around here.

He pulled his rental car into a spot in a small strip mall just north of the park. It was still early, maybe too early, to seek out the recipient of the message he carried. But he preferred to drive in the light traffic of the early morning, and it had only taken four hours to make the trip from Buffalo, even with the light snow.

He pitched himself forward so he could reach the wallet in his back pocket then withdrew the familiar folded envelope he'd tucked inside. He studied it one more time.

*Winnie* was all the scrawl on the front said. Otherwise, he might have mailed it—a soldier's last words to his wife—rather than delivering it after the year he'd spent recovering and rehabilitating. The only other distinguishing marks were the fold lines where he'd tucked it into a pocket during his extraction—and later into his wallet for safekeeping. Sand and dust had outlined the shape of the key inside, and one drop of what might have been blood stained a corner. Whether the blood belonged to him or to the one who had entrusted him with the message, he didn't know.

The memories again threatened to flood his mind, but after a few deep breaths, he felt fine. Time had done its healing work, and the counseling and his faith had helped. Some soldiers he'd encountered at Walter Reed had more wounds on the inside; others bore scars on the outside. He was in the latter group, but in the year since the IED, he'd come to terms with the physical challenges he now faced, and his therapists had flattered him as their star pupil.

He rubbed his left thigh. "Lord, guide my steps."

Somewhere in this town, a widow named Winnie—Winifred maybe?—deserved one final message from her husband. He slid the folded envelope back into his wallet and tucked it into the deep side pocket of his fleece-lined jacket before hoisting himself out of the car.

He paused for a few seconds, holding on to the car, checking his balance. The air stung his cheeks but carried the enticing aroma of food and a few strains of music coming from the direction of the park he'd passed. His stomach rumbled in response. Maybe his journey would be short. Maybe someone he encountered there might know where to find this Winnie. If not, at least he could probably score a coffee and something to eat.

Amy sensed a definite air of expectancy permeating the crowd that thronged Barclay Square. People weren't there just to see what the groundhog had to say. After a long, hard winter, they'd gathered to root for an early spring, like sports fans cheering on their favorite teams.

Meanwhile, the Groundhog Days events seemed designed to celebrate all things winter, almost like a farewell celebration. The ice sculptors chipped away at their masterpieces and, nearby, a chainsaw artist eyed what looked like the better part of a tree that had been craned in earlier. A smiling, costumed groundhog mascot, with much more energy than the real thing had ever displayed, leaped around and cavorted with the tourists, pausing to take selfies. And at one corner of the park, a magician in a black tuxedo and green sequined vest performed card tricks and pulled quarters out of the ears of a few children who stopped to watch. His top hat lay upturned on the ground, presumably awaiting additional coinage from pleased spectators.

Amy poured two cups of hot chocolate and handed them off to the young couple waiting in front of her booth. She was plumping up the crocheted amigurumi toy groundhogs so they'd be more visible to passersby when a sudden shadow appeared over the display.

"Can I help you?" She looked up.

The new customer was already taking in the display of muffins and pastries. When he glanced in her direction, Amy noticed his smile and how it spread over his whole face, creating little crinkles at the corners of his eyes. His eyebrows were a little on the bushy side but seemed to fit his dark, wavy hair. Definitely Italian.

"Chanan Home?" he asked, already collecting an armful of baked goods.

"It's a home for the developmentally disabled," Amy said.

"And the kiddos need a new roof or something, and you're raising money for them. Tale as old as time."

Amy laughed and found herself twirling a lock of hair. "Not a new roof," she said. "And they're not exactly kids. All the residents are between eighteen and thirtyish. Most of the money goes for enrichment experiences. Trips to the museum, ball games. Things like that."

"Sounds like a worthy cause." By this time, his collection of baked goods had grown so large a cupcake tumbled out of his grasp and landed in the snow. "It's okay," he said, bending to retrieve it. "Landed right side up."

"Would you like a box for those?"

"Nah, gonna eat them here."

"All of—" Amy stopped, not wishing to be impolite.

He chuckled. "Built up an appetite on the drive from Buffalo. And I braved quite the gauntlet to make it this far." He gestured to the crowds behind him. "And could I have two coffees?"

Amy turned to fill his order, and by the time she turned back with two steaming cups, he had started eating his second muffin. He reached for one of the coffees but pushed the other toward her. "May I buy the lady a coffee?"

Amy laughed but took a sip. "What do you do in Buffalo?" she asked. "Competitive eating?"

His wide grin sent those eye crinkles to punctuate a set of twinkling brown eyes. "Actually, I'm a meteorologist."

"For a television station?"

"No. I'm more into the science of meteorology. Not sure I could be a television weathercaster. TV stations these days, it seems, are just looking for a pretty face and someone who can pronounce 'precipitation.' I don't think that's for me."

"Oh, I could *totally* see you on television." It took two seconds for the import of what she had said to register, and when it did, Amy could feel the blood rush to her cheeks.

But that smile flashed again, and if she wasn't mistaken, he seemed to be blushing too, all the way to the tips of his ears. Or maybe it was just the freezing air.

A slightly hunched, middle-aged woman broke the spell, pushing her way to the table, juggling a notebook, a large camera, and an unfolded map. A frizz of brown hair mingled with a hint of gray jutted out from under her knitted cap. Her full cheeks flushed with exertion, and puffs of mist streamed from her mouth. "Can you tell me where to find the...Cherry Tree Inn?" She peered over her glasses, awaiting a response.

Amy braced herself. "Woodstock, Illinois."

"What?" The flustered woman dropped the map.

"I hope you don't have reservations," the man teased as he retrieved the map for her.

The tourist raised an arm to him like a conductor silencing the off-key French horn section. "*What* is it doing in Illinois?"

"You're asking about the bed-and-breakfast from the movie, right?" Amy asked.

The woman nodded.

"They filmed most of the movie in Woodstock, Illinois. Something about being closer to a production studio in Chicago."

"Oh!" She stopped to take a picture of a nearby brick hotel, looming a block away. "That would be the Pennsylvania Hotel, right?"

"Sorry." Amy winced.

"Then where's the Pennsylvania Hotel? Don't tell me that's in Illinois."

Amy pinched her lips together.

The woman sighed. "Seriously?"

Amy watched the tourist shuffle away, her shoulders slouched. Despite her disappointment, she still managed to snap several pictures.

Behind Amy, raucous sounds announced the arrival of Winnie and her crew. Each resident who was physically able carried more baked goods, even Violet, who clutched a box on her lap while one of Winnie's part-time aides pushed her all-terrain wheelchair.

"Here come my reinforcements." Amy helped unload the boxes they'd brought, and Winnie conferred with the aide over the schedule. Two of the residents, David and Melanie, would help Winnie at the booth first, while the aide accompanied the other three, taking in all the sights and sounds the event had to offer.

"I can count money," David said, pulling a chair up to the table and looking pleased with himself. "I count money at work all the time and clean tables and help customers."

Melanie shyly hovered close to Winnie.

With the new arrivals settled, Amy turned to her hungry customer. He'd whittled his pile of baked goods down to one cinnamon roll.

"Speaking of counting money," Amy said, "were you planning to pay for all that?"

He shoved the last bite of cinnamon roll into his mouth and mumbled, "Pay for what?" He lifted up his empty hands and backed away two steps.

"You wouldn't…"

"It's your word against mine, come to think of it. You don't have any tangible evidence that I ate anything," he teased, his smile never failing as he licked frosting from his upper lip. "So, what are you going to do about it?"

"I might just have to call a police officer."

"You'd do that?" He batted thick lashes.

"She'd do that!" David said.

"Well, in that case..." He reached for his back pants pocket, then his eyebrows rose. A second later, relief flooded his face. "That's right, I put it in my..." He shoved his hand into his right coat pocket then his left before those eyebrows rose again.

"You have *got* to be kidding me," Amy said.

"But I had it right here. I put it in my coat pocket when I got out of the car. I would never—"

He left the last bit unsaid as he and Amy studied each other.

"Better call a police officer," David said.

## Chapter Two

Guy retraced his steps to the car, hoping he'd merely dropped his wallet and he'd spot it lying in the snow somewhere. But there was no sign of it. Even as he checked the ground on the way back to the booth, he prayed that if he'd dropped it, a Good Samaritan would find it.

He could not, however, figure out how it could have escaped the deep pockets of his coat without help. The crowd was already closely packed when he arrived at the park. He'd paused to watch a couple of demonstrations and pushed in to check out the wares on several tables, and he'd been jostled multiple times. A thief might have taken advantage of his heavy winter wear and his distraction and lifted his wallet.

"Any luck?" the young woman said as he approached the booth again.

He shook his head. "Maybe I should go find that police officer."

"The police station is close by. I'll show you." She slid around the table to the front of the booth. "My name's Amy, by the way." She held out her gloved hand.

Guy reached and shook it. "Guy. You really don't have to come with me."

"That's okay. It's not far," Amy said. Her tone seemed friendly enough, but Guy couldn't help but wonder if she believed him about his missing wallet or if she intended to report him as a thief.

The crowd in the park threatened to separate them, so he offered her his arm and she took it. "If I'd known something like that could happen, I'd never have teased you," he said. But something about her had called for teasing. Like his kid sister.

"I wish I'd taken the time to set up one of those pay apps on my phone," he continued. "I guess I could see if my sister can wire money. I think they still do that. I might even have enough loose change in my car to pay for all those baked goods I scarfed down." Maybe. He'd been quite the glutton, and he had no idea why. What a fool he'd made of himself! He began to smile at that thought.

His smile froze before it fully developed. His own petty problems aside, how could he have lost the envelope?

He had to get it back.

He glanced over at her as they walked. Waves of auburn hair peeked out from her knitted hat. An intricately woven scarf, artfully arranged around her neck and shoulders, brought out the blue in her eyes. To be frank, with all the winter gear and the heavy coat and boots, he couldn't see much of her, but when a pixie-like smile swept across her face and her eyes lit up, he felt compelled to draw out that smile again.

And again. Okay, maybe not exactly like his kid sister.

They exited the park and crossed the street, where another crowd lined up next to a sprawling complex. They gave this queue a wide berth. The crowds of tourists had finally thinned out when he spotted the giant groundhog statue dressed in blue police gear holding the leads of a smaller K-9 statue.

"Is it a rule that all government buildings here have large groundhog statuary?" he asked.

"Well, not a rule, per se. But most do. There's a firefighter groundhog on the other side. And then there are businesses and schools...and churches. I think the chamber of commerce has a full tally, but I lost count."

He half expected her to head back to the park, but when he pulled the glass door open, she entered the station ahead of him.

A clerk behind a wall of plexiglass looked up at the onrush of frigid air. "Is it an emergency?"

"Just reporting a lost wallet," Guy said. "I hoped maybe somebody—"

She shook her head. "Sorry. Nothing turned in recently." She gestured to a line of uncomfortable-looking chairs. "I'll have someone come to take your statement as soon as they're free."

Guy and Amy wiped the snow off their boots the best they could on the already slushy mat then took seats in the small waiting area. The area was no-frills, with cement block walls painted in semi-gloss beige almost the same color as the floor.

"This doesn't look good," Amy said, gesturing to the other side of the plexiglass. Two desks were staffed by uniformed officers, each sitting opposite a varied collection of tourists.

At one desk, a young couple sat close together, arms entwined. Newlyweds? Guy wondered. Did people honeymoon in Punxsutawney? At the other desk, a harried father and mother tried to communicate with an officer while corralling three rambunctious kids.

"Pickpocket," the clerk said. "There's been a rash of them."

Guy felt his heart quicken its pace. "Has this happened before?"

The clerk shook her head. "New to me."

A moment later, the family rose to leave, and the officer who'd taken their statement ushered them back to the waiting area. "And are you staying nearby, in case we recover anything?"

"We're at the Woodlands Bed-and-Breakfast," the father said. "In Panic."

Guy turned to Amy. "They're panicked?" he whispered.

"Panic is the name of a—well, I guess they call it an unincorporated community, nine miles outside of Punxsutawney."

"Must be a story behind that name," he said.

"Not one everyone can agree on."

The family made quick work of bundling their children up for the cold and tramped out the door. Moments later, the young couple also exited.

"All right," the clerk said, and as Guy and Amy rose, she buzzed them in and pointed the way to the desk the couple had vacated.

"Pickpocket?" the officer asked, shuffling forms around on his desk. When Guy nodded, the officer said, "Our thief must have a type."

"What do you mean?" Guy asked. He waited for Amy to sit, then he dropped into the other chair before he realized the chairs were so close together, he had nowhere to put his left arm.

"Newlyweds," the officer said.

"Oh, we're not..." Guy shuffled uncomfortably and slid his chair a few inches away from Amy's.

"We're not a couple," Amy added, sliding hers even farther away.

The requisite forms took about ten minutes as Guy filled in all the pertinent details about the content of his wallet: credit cards, driver's license, his VIC, or veteran's ID card, and a little over two hundred dollars in cash. "One other thing," he started then paused.

The officer looked up. "Valuable?"

Guy bit his lower lip then took a deep breath. "An envelope."

Amy listened as Guy described the missing envelope and how he'd obtained it. An explosion, a dying comrade's last words to his wife, a key placed inside, and that single drop of blood. She could almost picture it all happening as Guy spoke. The huskiness creeping into his voice only emphasized the importance of what he'd lost.

Feeling as if she was intruding on something personal, she excused herself to find a restroom, at least long enough to get control of her own feelings. What now? Sure, he'd be okay if she just returned to the booth and left him in the excellent care of the Punxsutawney Police. But if Guy didn't want her to leave, she would stay. He'd had a rough morning already. She took a moment as she washed her hands to pray for him. Memories of the previous Sunday's sermon on the Good Samaritan and how he aided a stranger who fell among thieves seemed a pretty clear confirmation from God that she might help in some way.

"Here's a form you'll need to replace your missing driver's license," the officer was saying as Amy regained her seat. He shoved a sheet of paper in Guy's direction. "No driving, I'm afraid, until you replace it. There are computers at the library. You should be able to print a temporary from your state's DMV website."

"My car is parked in a strip mall. They won't tow it, will they?"

The officer sucked on his lower lip. "Give me the make and model, and we'll make sure it stays until you can legally drive again."

"What do you think the chances are?" Guy asked. "Of recovering anything?"

The officer trained his gaze on the pages in front of him. "I've got to level with you. Not good." He looked up. "You should cancel the credit cards and close any accounts the thief could access. We've got a couple of guys in plainclothes right now, milling with the crowd, trying to get a line on our guy, but our chances of recovering any of it are low."

Guy squirmed in his chair.

"That being said," the officer continued, "the wallet itself and the envelope you describe have no value to our thief, and he's not going to want to be caught with them in his possession. There's always a possibility he'll dump them somewhere, and they could be recovered that way."

"Dump them where?" Guy leaned forward.

"Public trash cans. Dumpsters." The officer tapped his pencil several times on the desktop. "Even a ditch by the side of a road, although if he's got any sense, he's going to want to get the cash out quick and dispose of the rest right away, so somewhere nearby. We haven't had this problem before, so my gut says it's a pro from out of town who decided to blend with the tourists and take advantage of the crowds."

"And if it's an amateur?" Guy asked.

The officer shrugged. "Then he'd be more unpredictable, make more mistakes." He stood. "Where are you staying, in case we find anything?"

Guy and Amy rose, following his cue.

"I hadn't actually planned on staying," Guy said. "I guess I'll have to find a hotel..."

He trailed off, and Amy discerned why. How could he pay for a hotel with no money or credit cards?

The officer shook his head. "Without reservations, I'm afraid everything is booked up ahead of Groundhog Day."

Guy tucked the officer's business card into his pocket. "I'll... uh...call you when I figure something out."

---

The clouds had lifted and the sun peeked out, but Guy felt even more chilled as they stepped out of the police station.

"What are you going to do?" Amy asked.

He stuffed his hands into his pockets. "I think I need to hang around a few more days, maybe poke around a few trash cans. Do some dumpster diving." He wrinkled his nose, and Amy laughed.

"I'm glad someone is finding this amusing," he said.

She flinched. "Sorry, nervous reflex. Of course, it's terrible. But your face when you..."

He smiled at her. "I think I'd also like to watch the crowds. I know they have officers out trying to catch the guy in action, but that's a lot of people to watch, and another set of eyes never hurts. I'm pretty observant."

"But you don't have a hotel. I still don't understand how a meteorologist comes all the way to Punxsutawney and doesn't plan to stay for the big day."

He set his jaw. "Four years undergrad work in meteorology, plus all that additional air force training, then six years predicting weather in some of the most extreme, unforgiving climates, with lives dependent on my efforts, and yet the world prefers its weather forecasts based on the predilections of a smelly rodent roughly the size of a housecat."

Amy inhaled. Or maybe she gasped. "Well, he's not that smelly, but when you put it that way... Where will you stay?"

He took three more steps before answering. "I guess there's always my car."

She caught up to him and clutched his arm. "You can't sleep in your car. It's freezing." As if to prove her point, her breath clouded up between them.

He raised his shoulders in a slow shrug. "I'll figure something out." He started back toward the park again. Cheerful polka music had begun, almost mocking him, a stark contradiction to his somber mood.

"Well," Amy said, "I know there's an extra bed at the group home. I can ask Winnie if you can stay there."

He whirled around. "Winnie?"

"Yeah, she's my friend who actually runs the group home. I just have to check with her."

"Winnie"—he grabbed both her upper arms—"was the name on the envelope."

# Chapter Three

Instead of returning to the booth, Amy took Guy's arm and steered him toward the bank of food trucks. "You hungry?" she asked. "I'm hungry." Although in truth she wasn't certain if it was hunger or pangs of apprehension that the day was about to get even more difficult.

"Wait!" Guy said. "Shouldn't we go talk to Winnie?"

She reached for his arm again and dragged him to the food trucks. "You and I have a couple of things to talk about. We don't even know it's the same Winnie. First, maybe we should try to figure that out in a way that doesn't disrupt her whole life. So, are you hungry?"

"Well, I shouldn't be," he said. "And besides, I have no cash. What do you mean, 'disrupt'?"

"Long story. Lunch is on me." She joined the short line for a truck offering hot dogs, cheese fries, and steak sandwiches. "Hot dog okay?"

Although a quizzical expression dominated his face, he managed to nod, so she ordered two hot dogs and an order of cheese fries to share, since the portion carried away by the customer ahead of her looked large enough to serve a family of five. They didn't speak until they'd loaded on their condiments, listening instead to the sound of sizzling steak and the hearty chorus of fries being dropped into vats of hot oil. They found seats near the firepit where several impatient children tried to toast marshmallows, every attempt turning into a smoking soot ball.

She'd scarfed down half her hot dog before Guy hazarded a comment.

"You have to admit," he said, "it feels pretty providential that the first person I come across after arriving in Punxsutawney actually even knows someone named—"

"You can't tell her."

He looked up. Those crinkles she had admired earlier had disappeared from his eyes.

She took a few moments to frame her next words. "Winnie told me about her ex. There's a lot of history there. Why drag up all those feelings again? Especially now that you have no message to give her?"

"Ex?" Guy said. "Maybe it's not the same Winnie. I'm pretty hazy about a few details from that day, but I clearly remember him saying, 'Give this to my *wife* in Punxsutawney.'"

"And all it said on the envelope was Winnie? No last name, no address?"

Guy paused, closing his eyes as if composing himself. "Not that he was able to finish." Silence ensued for the better part of a minute. "So, he was her ex?"

"*If* she's the Winnie you're looking for, they were separated, but I don't think she ever actually divorced him." Amy stared at the firepit. "But how many Winnies can there be in Punxsutawney? It's not a big town, and Winifred isn't exactly a common name these days." She reached for a cheese fry. "What was *his* last name?" she asked before popping a fry into her mouth.

Guy stared off into the crowd for a moment then looked back, shaking his head. "That's one of the details I'm hazy about. He was a replacement driver, assigned at the last minute. I'm sure he told me his name. For some reason, I'm thinking it was presidential."

"Well, Winnie's is Franklin, and Benjamin Franklin was never president. Unless you count first names. Then there's Franklin Pierce and Franklin Delano Roosevelt. If that's how your mind works."

"I was pretty concussed myself at the time. Not sure how well my mind was working."

They ate in silence for a few minutes before Guy spoke again. "Winnie's husband, or her ex, whatever… He *was* in the military, right?"

"Not that she ever mentioned," Amy said. "All I know is that he left her. Deserted her, really. It's left her awfully bitter."

"Maybe you'd better tell me the whole story."

---

Amy paused to lick a bit of melted cheese from her thumb. "It all happened before I met her," she began. "It's what we bonded over—the whole stereotype of girlfriends commiserating over the rats who dumped them."

"This is something that women actually do?"

"Oh, for sure. The process usually involves copious amounts of ice cream. She had it lots worse than I did. She'd married her rat. They weren't together a year before he took off, and he couldn't have picked a worse time. She was balancing debt from college and the wedding, the stress of a new marriage, all while trying to finish her master's in social work. Then came the cancer diagnosis."

Guy didn't interrupt her story. He leaned toward the fire, resting his forearms on his knees.

"He stuck around for maybe three weeks after her surgery," she went on. "One of her first days out of the house, she met with her academic advisor, to try to work out a plan to catch up. When she returned home, he was just gone. All his clothes from his closet. Any money they had in their apartment. He even took some of her grandma's jewelry."

Guy tried to remember his driver. Had he seemed like the type to desert a sick wife? "It must have been difficult for both of them, you know, dealing with such a serious illness in that first year."

Amy's jaw dropped. "I can't believe you would take his side."

"I'm not taking anyone's side, just trying to see the whole picture. It's a huge trial for a relationship still in its early days. People vow 'for better or worse,' and they're sincere in their intentions to weather life's storms together. Someday. They don't expect the storm to hit before the honeymoon is properly over."

"You speaking from experience?"

"Never quite made it to the altar. Did pop the question though. Right before I deployed."

"Long distance relationships can be difficult."

"That part we managed just fine," Guy said. "We talked online as much as we could. To be fair to Lucinda, we'd only been dating a few months, and I had my doubts, even before I bought the ring." He still recalled her face, radiating concern, when she'd shown up at his bedside at Walter Reed. Day by day she came, tried to cheer him, and helped him with his rehab. And day by day the love faded from her eyes until only duty remained. She'd cried when he suggested she go home, that they break things off, but he could see the relief mingled with her tears.

Guy shook off his own feelings to concentrate on the matter at hand. "Winnie's husband didn't leave a note? Never tried to contact her? Nobody ever came to inform her of his death?"

"You mean someone in uniform, with a flag and all that?" Amy shook her head. "No, nothing. So maybe it *wasn't* her husband who died. Maybe there *is* another Winnie in Punxsy."

"Or maybe he never informed the military he was married," Guy said. "Do you know if she still has a picture of him? I'd know him if I saw him." The man's face was one detail that had engraved itself on his brain.

Amy thought for a moment. "She kept her wedding pictures. She always said that she'd paid for the dress, the flowers, and the photos, so she kept them as a reminder to never make that mistake again."

Guy sighed. "That does sound bitter."

"She's hurt," Amy said. "I don't know. Maybe it's a good thing that envelope was stolen. Maybe it would be better not to rip open those old wounds."

"That's not up to us," Guy said. "A dying soldier took the very last bit of his life to say something to his wife. I owe it to him to do my best to see that she gets his message."

"And you have no idea what it said? No peeking?"

He set his jaw. "That was sacrosanct. Only between them. Even if it's not pleasant, she deserves to know."

Amy stared into the fire for a few moments. "Assuming she's the right Winnie and that we find the envelope."

"We?"

"Winnie's my friend. I want to help. I can keep my eyes peeled and poke through trash, just like you. And I bet I can also think of some pretext for her to dig out those wedding photos of hers."

---

Despite the seriousness of the conversation, the polka band lured Amy's attention. A big tuba *oompahed* away, while a clarinetist got a workout, her fingers flying as she executed a series of well-practiced runs, trills, and glissandos. Two accordions filled in the rest. Several couples, most elderly, kept time to the music on the wooden dance floor, just like her German grandfather had taught her. She had memories of standing on his feet at some cousin's wedding while they twirled around the room.

"Well, maybe after the morning we've had, we need something to shake off a bit of the gloom, maybe get the blood pumping."

"Huh?"

"Do you polka?" Amy asked, holding out her hand in invitation.

Guy jerked his head, as if startled. "I...sorry, no."

She didn't know whether he had even seen her outstretched hand, so she quickly brought it down to her thigh and wiped it on her jeans, as if to clean off what felt like a rebuff.

"I really just need to cancel those credit cards." He took out his cell phone.

Amy left him sitting on the bench while she went back to the booth. During a lull in business, she pulled up a chair next to Winnie's.

"I saw you and that handsome new friend of yours spending some time together at the fire," Winnie said. "It kind of looked like marshmallows weren't the only thing you wanted s'more of," she teased.

Amy elbowed her friend. "I don't know that you can even call him my friend yet. He's just a tourist down on his luck."

"Ah, then you *do* think he's handsome."

Amy looked away, whether to hide the warmth creeping into her cheeks or that idiotic smile she could feel on her face, she wasn't sure. "Maybe let's drop the subject. He's not going to be in town long, and he doesn't seem all that interested in me, anyway."

"Uh-huh," Winnie said. "Spoil all my fun. And what did the police say?"

"Just that he's not the only victim. Meanwhile, he doesn't exactly have a place to stay, even if he could afford one. Could he use your extra room? He's a veteran, and he seems like an all-right guy." Even if he didn't polka.

But Winnie was already wagging her head. "Love to help you there, but it's not permitted. I can't allow someone to stay unless they've been properly vetted."

"I didn't think about that." Amy templed her fingers in front of her lips. "I don't know what to do. Poor guy mentioned sleeping in his car."

"You do have that pullout sofa in your shop," Winnie said.

"I can't have him stay with me. That doesn't seem…proper."

"Your loft locks, right? And as you said, he seems like an all-right guy."

Amy took a long breath. "I suppose."

"And a veteran." Winnie leaned closer. "And very handsome."

Amy gave her friend a playful shove.

Winnie squealed as she lost her balance and her chair tipped into the snow.

Amy tried to fight back laughter, but failed miserably, at least until Winnie's fluffy snowball hit her in the face.

---

The winter sun already hung low in the sky when Guy forced his frame into the front seat of Amy's little Civic. Whether he would fit was only one of his misgivings.

He'd sat in the park for hours, staring at strangers, until he could no longer feel his right foot, and he'd seen nothing more suspicious than a little girl tell her mother that she hadn't had a treat all day—while remnants of cotton candy clung to her face. He'd poked through enough trash cans that he felt just as sticky as those pink cheeks. Maybe trying to find the pickpocket or recover the envelope would prove to be a fool's errand.

"Are you sure I won't be in the way?" he asked.

"Not at all," she said. "I only have one more class tonight, and then the shop is closed until after Groundhog Day. Besides, I want to help, and how else are you going to find out if you even have the right Winnie?"

"I just—"

"Hate to depend on anyone? Everyone needs help sometimes."

"I've had a few counselors tell me the same thing," he said. "But then they send you to occupational therapy so you can manage on your own, so kind of mixed messages there, right?"

He took in the hilly scenery as it shifted from small city to town, to suburbia, then finally to rural. They turned at a road sign pointing to Panic, which also pointed the way to the more promising-sounding towns of Paradise and Desire. A hand-painted addition to the sign advertised the way to a buggy shop. Aside from sporadic evidence of horse-drawn conveyances, the road was mostly lined with dingy drifts of plowed snow, with an occasional red barn or boarded-up farmstand interrupting the white-blanketed fields.

A horse and buggy passed them on the road coming the other way, and Amy pumped her brakes. Guy thought the move precautionary, but after the buggy passed in a cacophony of clopping hooves, she steered the car left into a driveway that opened up into a parking area stretching between a large white farmhouse and a brick-red barn. He didn't realize the barn was her shop until he saw the painted sign with the knitting cartoon sheep and the name GOT EWE UNDER MY SKEIN.

He groaned. "Clever name."

"Then why does everyone groan?" she asked as she pushed open her door.

"Puns can be an acquired taste. Memorable though."

It took him a little longer to shift his leg out of the car, and he hoped she didn't notice. After all that walking and sitting in the cold, even the muscles and joints in his right leg were stiff. By the time he joined her at the trunk, she'd managed to unload almost everything herself. He took his bags from her.

"You have quite a bit for someone who didn't plan to stay," she said.

"I was on my way to Philadelphia from here. Job interview."

"Oh, right. Meteorologist, but not for television. Is that what you did in the army?"

"Air force, actually," he said. "Meteorologists forecast when it's safe for the planes to fly and help predict sandstorms and other weather systems that could threaten missions."

"What would you be doing in Philadelphia?"

"Forecasting wind and sun potential for generating energy."

"Wouldn't that be kind of boring, considering what you're used to?" She turned the key in the commercial glass door built into the front of the barn and pulled it open.

"Boring can be underrated." He followed her in.

Overhead LED lights flicked on and then grew brighter, and he took a good look around. Wide planks finished in a weathered gray covered the floor. A black cat stood staring for a moment, eyes glittering, but then it blinked once and took off, skidding as it disappeared behind some shelving.

The walls were lined with shelves—wood crates stacked on their sides, really—filled with colorful yarn. Atop one of them, a large gray tabby napped. It opened its eyes and then, apparently satisfied the new arrivals posed no danger, let them droop back into slumber.

Exposed beams spanned the wood ceiling, and six rough posts added to their support. Each post was a display area for crochet hooks and knitting needles and a bunch of other paraphernalia Guy couldn't readily identify.

In the center of the room, as if it was a showpiece, sat a huge farmhouse table, its warm stain gleaming under the lights. A dozen or so chairs of varying vintages encircled it.

"Oh, wow," Guy said, running his hand along the pitted tabletop. "They don't make them like this anymore."

"I know," she said, taking a moment to stroke the table as well. "Someone just left it in the farmhouse. Can you believe it? But when we redid the kitchen, it didn't quite fit anymore, so it ended up here. Imagine how many stories it could tell. Family dinners, holidays, children pulled up to it doing their homework." She laughed. "You can still see the impressions of a few numbers and words indented into the wood. I think that only makes it more beautiful."

"For sure." He looked up and noticed her eyes were shining. Maybe it was the light.

Their silent eye contact lasted maybe just a beat too long. She headed past the table to a green plaid sofa, which faced a woodstove. "This is you," she said. "It opens up, but it might actually be more comfortable this way. It's not much, but it beats…"

"My car. Yes, I know, and I really appreciate this. Hopefully, it won't take long to recover the envelope and get some cash wired. I left a message with my sister, but then my phone died."

She showed him where he could charge it and then pointed out the half bath on the lower level. "My class is coming at seven. You hungry?"

Guy nodded before he realized she was headed toward a staircase half hidden behind a rough-hewn check-out station. She gestured for him to precede her, but he managed to croak out, "Ladies first."

At least she didn't race up the stairs, which gave him a chance to examine the pitch of the steps. Not bad, but he felt apprehensive at the sheer number of them looming ahead of him. He took a deep breath, used the handrails for added support and stability, then stepped up with his right leg, drew up his left, then led with his right again.

Partway up, the black cat came racing up the steps, and he clasped the railing with white knuckles, willing himself not to lose his balance. Once the adrenaline passed, he started taking the steps two at a time, leading with the right, then drawing up the left, so he wouldn't lag too far behind. By the time she arrived at the top of the stairs and turned around, he was almost there.

If she noticed his struggles, she didn't let on.

The loft took up about half the square footage of the shop below and kept much of the character with the exposed beams and wide plank floors. Instead of a woodburning stove, a gas fireplace flanked one wall. She flicked it on with a remote and beckoned him to sit down, refusing his offer of help.

The sound of the opening of a cat food can instantly drew the two cats, both rubbing against her ankles.

"The gray one is Cap'n Hook," she said. "He's my senior cat. We've been together for a while. The little black one is Stitch. She came to us last spring, probably searching for barn mice. They're already best buds. I hope you're not allergic."

"No, I'm good with cats." He looked around the rest of her loft. Nothing appeared ostentatious, frilly, or overtly feminine. She seemed to favor natural materials and comfortable decor. A Bible verse hung over the fireplace and framed pictures of family stood on the shelves on either side of it, along with a hodgepodge of timeworn books.

A well-worn Bible lay on the coffee table, and Guy ran his hand along the cover, its very presence encouraging him. His trip certainly wasn't going according to his own plan, but he thought it more than coincidental that the first person he came across after arriving in town was someone of faith. He remembered the prayer he'd breathed as he got out of the car. *Lord, guide my steps.* As disappointed as Guy was in his own inability to complete the mission that brought him there, he couldn't help but wonder if God had a different plan at work.

The gray tabby jumped up next to him, and Guy let the cat sniff his hand before tentatively petting his head. "Howdy, Cap'n." Introductions out of the way, the cat climbed into Guy's lap and settled in for another snooze. The black cat picked out a spot in front of the fireplace, arched her back, then curled up. Before long, the flickering flames, the radiating heat, the rhythmic purring of the cat, and the homey sounds coming from the kitchen threatened to lull him to sleep, especially after such a physically and emotionally trying day. His head bobbed.

"Two orders of groundhog soup, coming up," Amy said, setting two plates on the coffee table. Each plate contained two halves of a golden grilled cheese sandwich flanking a steaming bowl of soup.

"This looks great. How did you have time to make—wait, did you say *groundhog*?"

Amy laughed. "It's vegetable, actually. No groundhogs were harmed in the making of this soup. I'll tell you the story behind the name while we eat." She dropped into a chair next to him, picked up a spoon, then stopped. "I usually pray, if you don't mind."

"Why would I mind?" He bowed his head as she uttered a short, simple prayer.

"So," he said, lifting a spoonful of soup for closer examination, "you said there was a story?"

"The recipe came from Winnie. She called it her 'Busy Day Vegetable Soup' recipe, and she submitted it to her church cookbook. But they turned it down, saying they already had too many vegetable soup recipes. Would she care to submit a different kind?

"But Winnie was partial to this one, so she added an ingredient: 'one pound ground groundhog, browned and drained, *optional*' at the beginning of the recipe. And at the end, she put a note saying it's even better without the groundhog."

Guy laughed. "And I bet they took it, no questions asked."

"Never batted an eye," Amy said. "Anyway, it's quick and easy. Almost everything is from a can or the freezer. A few of the residents know how to make it themselves."

They chatted during the rest of the meal, and Guy jumped when a bell sounded. He sent a wide-eyed glance to the clock. How had so much time passed so quickly?

"Time for my class," she said, taking one last sip of her water. "Coming?"

"You cooked. How about I clean up?" he asked. "I'll join you there."

He made quick work of it, leaving her dishwasher humming as he carefully maneuvered the stairs. Going downstairs had been harder for him to master, for some reason, and he was glad to do it without an audience.

Eight people sat around the farmhouse table, Amy on her feet circling them, stopping to observe and help as needed.

"We have a late arrival," she sang out, and all the faces turned to look at him. He recognized three from the group home. Next to them, two gray-headed women whispered to each other. A gaunt middle-aged woman wearing a turban and two younger women, one still with remnants of acne on her chin and forehead, completed the group. The youngest looked up at him curiously then turned to focus on her work in her lap.

"Oh, I don't knit," he said.

"Crochet!" the group cried out, almost in unison, then laughed at their own chorus.

"Oh!" he said. "Sorry, don't do that either."

"Well, this is my advanced amigurumi class." Amy must have read his puzzled look. "Those little crocheted dolls. They're all the rage on the internet."

"Carry on then. I'll just watch. Unless you'd like me to light a fire?" He tipped his head toward the woodstove.

"Sounds heavenly!" the turbaned woman answered.

When Amy nodded, he went to work. He preferred the top-down method, so he laid two larger logs parallel at the bottom, then smaller logs, kindling, and finally a little bit of newspaper on top. He lit it with a long fireplace match and nursed the flame while he listened to the group chatting. The turbaned woman shared about her latest bout of chemo, and the group home members talked excitedly about the big day they had in the park. The two older women kept whispering, but not softly enough to keep their gossip hidden. Apparently, they thought he was handsome, and he resembled a German family nearby. The girl with the acne, the one Amy addressed as Olivia, just kept to herself, her crochet hook constantly moving.

He eased himself back onto the sofa, listening to the voices and watching the flames, until sleep overtook him.

# Chapter Four

Amy preferred the older, drip-style coffee makers. Something about the smell of a pot of coffee filling her loft really made it feel like home. While she waited for it to finish, she'd flipped on the television to catch the news and weather. They predicted "nuisance snow" without much accumulation, so it shouldn't impact her day much.

She paused to consider the weathercaster, wondering how much he understood of what he read from a script. Yeah, she could totally see Guy on television.

When the coffee finished, she poured two cups then put them and a small collection of yesterday's leftover pastries onto a tray before tiptoeing down the stairs.

Guy had fallen asleep long before her class ended. Instead of waking him, she'd merely draped a blanket on him, leaving an extra one and a pillow next to him in case he woke up cold in the night after the fire had died.

All was quiet below, so she thought he might still be sleeping, but as she reached the bottom of the stairs, she saw that all the lights were on. She didn't see him though. Maybe he'd gone out. A moment later, he emerged from the bathroom with a bag of toiletries in his hand.

"Good morning." She handed him a coffee cup then slid the rest of the tray on the table. "For a second there, I thought you might have gone for an early morning run. Isn't that something you military types do?" The words had barely passed her lips before she remembered his limp.

"Not today," he said. "Not in quite a while, in fact." He pulled out a chair at the table and busied himself with his coffee. "What about you? Do you run?"

"It depends entirely on what's chasing me," she quipped, anxious to change the subject. She pointed to his cell phone, still on its charger. "Anything from your sister?"

He picked it up and poked through a few screens. "Nothing. I'm beginning to think she might be traveling. She said something about a cruise, but I thought it was later in the month."

"No one else at home you could try?"

He shook his head. "Never knew my dad, really. We lost Mom a couple of years ago."

"I'm sorry."

He shrugged. "I can try to get a new bank card or credit card expedited to me. Not sure I can prove my identity without my driver's license."

"You still want to keep looking for the pickpocket too, right?"

He nodded. "That shindig still going on at the park?"

"For several more days," she said. "Today I'm going to Lunch with Phil. And I have tickets for Gobbler's Knob's Got Talent."

"Gobbler's Knob's got..." His face looked like he was trying to translate that from Martian.

"Gobbler's Knob is where the groundhog makes his prediction. There's a big talent show in town today, and the winner will be announced on Groundhog Day at Gobbler's Knob. And then there's the big ball tomorrow."

"Ball?"

"Yes, it's a popular event. Everyone gets all gussied up. A lot of tourists will be mingling around. You're in luck because I have two tickets to everything, courtesy of the chamber of commerce."

He drained the last of his coffee. "Good thinking. Thief will probably go where the crowds are. Prime hunting ground for our pickpocket."

"Got a suit?"

Guy stood outside the yarn shop and tried calling his sister one more time. Again, no answer. The credit card company was no help. Oh, they'd canceled his card easily enough, but they balked at sending a new one anywhere except his address on file. The bank proved only marginally more helpful, suggesting what sounded like a doubtful process of establishing his identity at a local branch and *perhaps* getting to his money that way.

In the meantime, he found himself depending on the kindness of strangers, which wasn't as bad as he thought it might be. Amy seemed enthusiastic to team up, as if they were embarking on some grand adventure, so she didn't make him feel as if he was imposing or intruding too much. Except she seemed to include him in this planned lunch with somebody named Phil, and he had no intention of becoming a third wheel as she ate with some boyfriend. He would make himself scarce.

He looked down at the assorted tire tracks in the snow outside the shop—including one set of bicycle tracks. It didn't seem like she did much business. Besides the class last night, where one woman bought a new crochet hook, he hadn't seen her make any money. A yarn shop in a barn on a country road in the middle of nowhere didn't seem like the greatest business plan. He wondered how she could support herself, much less him, albeit temporarily. He needed to pay back her kindness and get out of her hair as quickly as possible.

But accessing his funds was only part of his problem. He still needed to learn more about this Winnie. He surveyed the farmhouse with the group home van parked alongside. The quantity of footprints connecting the two buildings suggested regular contact, which *should* give him an opportunity to see her again. But to ask to look at her wedding album? That would take some Amy magic.

Amy might be right about another thing. Did it make sense to tell Winnie about the existence of the envelope with zero chance of her ever reading that final message?

Was the envelope even recoverable? He closed his eyes and tried to imagine if he were a thief, picking pockets for ready cash and finding that envelope.

What would he do?

That was easy. He'd return it. He shook his head. Yeah, he'd make a terrible thief.

But would a more hardened criminal toss it, along with anything else not immediately spendable? Or would it intrigue him? Might he open the envelope and read the letter inside? The thought made Guy shudder.

And what about the key? Did the letter explain its significance? If the key led to something valuable, the thief might hang on to it.

Guy took a deep, bracing breath of cold air with a hint of woodsmoke. He hoped the letter hadn't been charred to ashes, its message disappearing in a haze and carried by the prevailing westerlies, swirling through barren tree branches.

Enough of a sliver of hope remained that he owed it to Winnie and to his driver to search for a few more days. He pulled out his cell phone, dialed the HR manager in Philadelphia, and postponed his job interview a few days.

"Yes, we can reschedule." The voice on the phone hesitated. "But you need to know that we're interviewing other strong candidates. There's no guarantee the job will still be around."

He thanked her and stuffed his phone back into his pocket. He didn't have time to ruminate. He held the door open for Amy as she handed him another coffee in a to-go cup before she locked up the shop behind her.

"Yes, I know where that bank branch is," Amy said as she pulled her car into the same strip mall parking lot where Guy had left his car. "We'll have to hoof it today, I'm afraid. Parking is difficult this time of year. I have one stop to make first, then I'll show you where the bank is."

She watched out of the corner of her eye as he climbed out of her car. She worried a little about all the walking and his limp, but he managed deftly and didn't seem as stiff as he'd been last night.

Together, they hit the sidewalk and headed in the direction opposite the park. Cars with out-of-state plates navigated the street, mixed with many from Pennsylvania and the occasional yellow school bus. They passed a strip of fast-food places, some with their own smiling groundhog statuary ready to welcome guests. Cars lined their drive-throughs, each emitting a cloud of white fog from its tailpipe into the chilly air.

Guy craned his neck as they passed.

"You can't be hungry," she teased.

"Just noticing all those dumpsters. How easy would it be for the pickpocket to take cash out to pay for food and then dump the wallet out with his trash? The letter could be sitting in one of them right now."

"Also an easy way of being spotted. If I saw someone throw a wallet away, I'd be suspicious. I doubt he'd dump it someplace quite that public."

"I hope you're right." He picked up his pace to catch up with her.

Less than ten minutes after leaving the parking lot, she veered off toward the tailor's shop, and Guy rushed ahead of her to open the door.

Unlike some of the more modern edifices they passed, this shop was in a converted two-story residence painted in a peeling hunter green. Amy suspected the tailor still lived on the floors above. Most of the main floor had been converted to a collection of related businesses, probably added on when services for a tailor declined. A large rack of tuxes stood ready to rent in what originally must have been the dining room. The door to a small bedroom now sported a sign designating it as a fitting room. The former kitchen in the back, she knew, held racks and racks of used prom, bridesmaid, and ball gowns sold on consignment. She knew, because that was where she'd picked out the dress she'd bought for the Groundhog Ball.

Mr. Fisher, the elderly tailor, stood behind the counter, talking with a customer. He had a full head of wavy white hair combed into a style he'd probably sported for decades. Drooping lids nearly hooded his eyes. He wore a crisp, striped dress shirt, open at the neck and rolled up at the sleeves. His ears were the hugest Amy had ever seen, and she tried not to stare, instead casting her glance to Olivia, seated on a stool nearby, hand-stitching a hem.

"Hi, Miss Frye," Olivia almost whispered, setting her sewing aside. "Here for your dress?" Without waiting for an answer, she went to a small rack behind the counter and retrieved an opaque garment bag. "All hemmed and pressed, and I let the waist out a little for you," she said as she placed it on the counter. "Would you like to try it on?"

Amy could feel the heat envelop her cheeks.

Mr. Fisher cleared his throat. "Olivia, why don't you go downstairs and get some more garment bags. I'll take care of Amy."

Olivia bobbed her head, like some Victorian parlormaid, and popped off without a word.

"Sorry about that," Mr. Fisher said. "She sews like a dream, but she has no tact with the customers."

"She's awfully young," Guy said.

"Eighteen with thirty years' experience," he said. "Let me show you." He pulled up the bottom of the garment bag, revealing the hem of Amy's peacock-blue dress. "Look, such tiny stitches. Not a single pucker. I used to be able to do work like this, or maybe I flatter myself. I'm not sure what I'd do without her. Ex-Amish, you know."

He grabbed the yellow pencil he'd tucked behind his ear and started totaling up the numbers on Amy's receipt. "They teach 'em young. I'll bet she's been sewing since she was three. Have you seen the new groundhog mascot yet?"

Amy blinked at the non sequitur. "I think so. In the park yesterday."

"We made that." Mr. Fisher pointed to the stool where Olivia had sat. "Well, mostly she did. They planned to send away for a new one… from out of town." The man's nose grew red, a level of indignation rising in his voice, as if sourcing a groundhog costume from somewhere other than Punxsutawney would have been a crime against humanity. "But I told them no, we could do it. We'd always done it. But the pattern was gone, you see. Destroyed in the flood back in… when was that…'96, I think? So, you can see how much wear they got out of the thing. That's quality. Not going to find that on the internet. So we had to take the whole thing apart and start over."

Amy looked at the total and took her credit card out of her wallet. Once Mr. Fisher started on one of his stories, it could take a while.

"You always do such a fantastic job," she said. "They would have been foolish to go anywhere else." She ran her card through the swiper then drew a five from her pocket. "For Olivia," she said, setting the bill on the counter.

As she turned, she caught Guy inspecting the tuxes. She draped the garment bag over her arm and joined him. "Need anything for the ball?"

"Men don't wear tuxes to it, do they?"

"A few, maybe. A suit's okay though."

"Are you sure you want *me* to go?"

"What better place to catch a pickpocket in action, all those people milling around? Some celebrating *awhile*, if you know what I mean. Ladies leaving their purses on the tables while they dance. If I were a pickpocket, I'd be there for sure."

When he didn't respond, she asked, "Don't you want to go?"

He held the door open for her as they exited. "It's not that. It's…I mean, what about Phil? Will he be there?"

"Phil?" It took Amy a moment to realize who he meant. "Oh, Phil. He may put in an appearance, but it's a late night for him. He has a busy workload in front of him."

"But he won't have a problem with me…escorting you to the ball? I mean, it might look like…I mean others might think it's a date, and I'd hate to cause problems between you."

"Between me and Phil?" She did her best to cover her mischievous smile with a cough, then she took his arm as they continued down the sidewalk. "No, I doubt he'd notice. He has a lot on his mind right now."

A squeal went up from across the street, and Amy watched as two teen girls leaned in close to pose for a pouty selfie with the cavorting groundhog mascot, his smile permanent behind those big buck teeth.

The bank was on the next block. Yet another smiling groundhog statue stood in front of the small branch to greet them.

The glass doors opened onto salt-stained wall-to-wall navy carpet. A cordon led to a line of teller stations constructed of blond wood and plenty of plexiglass. Amy read dog-eared magazines in a drafty waiting area shoehorned just to the right of the door while Guy was led past several cubicles—each also constructed of blond wood topped with clear plexiglass—into an identical cubicle at the end. Amy could see him shake hands with the bank representative, but when they sat down, only the tops of their heads were visible, and that view was refracted through several other glass walls first.

She had leafed through three magazines and considered covertly tearing out a recipe for a German potato salad made with sweet potatoes, when she realized she could take a picture instead, sparing the three-year-old periodical any further abuse. When she next looked up, Guy headed toward her.

"Any luck?" she asked.

He plopped into the chair next to her as if he'd just finished a marathon.

"Possibly. They need some kind of bank manager approval, and they'll also verify with the police department that I filed a report. And they took my picture to compare with the DMV records in New York. Earliest she thought they could get it would be tomorrow. I'll check again in the morning."

They retraced their steps, and Amy hung her dress in the back seat of her car, draping the long skirt across the seat before heading to Barclay Square. A local band had taken the stage, their music almost completely overtaken by the whine of a chain saw. Guy and Amy stopped to look at the artist's progress on his statue—a groundhog, of course—then they found a quieter spot on a bench overlooking much of the park.

Guy picked up a stick and poked through the adjacent trash can before joining her on the bench. He shrugged. "You never know."

"Maybe we're going about this all wrong," Amy said. "Do you remember anyone you encountered before you noticed your wallet missing?"

"Amy, there were tons of people. All strangers."

"Anyone unique? Maybe distracting?"

"It's *all* distracting. I didn't expect any of this, you know. I thought I'd be here way ahead of all this hoopla."

"Well, we're very good at hoopla around here." She adopted a mock defensive tone. "Hoopla takes time."

"I'm sure it does."

"And effort."

"Believe me, you all are the world champions of hoopla. This is amazing. But I thought I'd be here maybe a few hours, find Winnie, deliver the letter, then be on the road to Philly."

"Okay, let's take a step back. You drove down from Buffalo."

"Saw the crowds, parked my car. I figured someone in the park might know somebody named Winnie."

"So, you arrived at Barclay Square. Freeze the video. Who do you see?"

He closed his eyes. "Nameless, faceless strangers. Wait. I stopped to watch a magician. He wasn't very good. He pulled quarters out of kids' ears, but he wouldn't let the kids keep the quarters."

"And that's bad?"

"I don't know about you, but I have a very proprietary relationship with anything that comes out of my ears. The kids seemed to feel the same way."

"Did you get close to him?"

"I guess. He asked me to pick a card."

"Hmm."

"Hmm?"

"Anybody good at pulling quarters out of ears might also be good at pulling wallets out of pockets."

Guy bobbed his head from side to side, considering the matter. "Well, maybe, but I'm not sure he had that level of skill. Wait, there was someone else. I stood right next to a woman taking a lot of pictures of just about everything. You know her. She stopped by your booth asking about some bed-and-breakfast."

"Well, I don't know her, per se. We always get a few tourists in who are fans of the movie."

"And you're not?"

"Oh, we for sure are. In fact, they show it in the community center every year. But they're looking for places where the movie was filmed, and you get tired telling them those places aren't here. Do you remember anybody else?"

"Well, a pretty lady sold me some awesome baked goods."

"Which you haven't actually paid for yet."

"Yeah, working on that."

# Chapter Five

Guy didn't know what possessed him to admit that he thought Amy was pretty, especially when she was so clearly out of bounds. Or maybe that was why he felt safe to do so. He wasn't looking for a relationship, and she was already involved with this Phil, so it seemed like a perfect safety net. A couple of days of harmless banter, and then he would be off for that interview.

She glanced at her fitness tracker. "Time to head for lunch."

"With Phil?" he said. "Look, I don't want to be a third wheel. How about I stay here and keep an eye out for our pickpocket? Maybe rummage through a little more trash."

"You've hit every trash can in the park at least three times. Come on." Her whole face lit up. "You have to meet Phil."

What harm could it do? Overcome by that smile, he followed her to her car.

The drive didn't take long, but the area already felt rural again by the time they entered the gates of Gobbler's Knob.

"Isn't this where the groundhog sees its shadow?"

"Yup. This lunch is an annual event."

"And Phil will be here too?"

That bewitching smile hit him again, with a hint of mischief in it this time.

"And I'm not intruding?"

"Not at all. In fact, I'll be glad to introduce you." She took his hand and led him into the event center and directly over to a crowded area of the room. In the back stood several men, their top hats the only things visible over the crowd. That seemed to be the direction Amy was pulling him. Maybe Phil was one of those guys.

Minutes later, a group in front of them departed, and she tugged him up to the top-hatted man who was holding a fat groundhog.

"Meet Phil," Amy said.

Guy became acutely aware that Amy was still holding his hand, so he pulled away quickly. He looked the slightly gray-headed man in the eyes, held out his hand, and said, "Hi, Phil."

Amy laughed. "That's not Phil." She leaned down to look at the groundhog. "Hi, Phil. This is my friend, Guy."

Guy leaned over and studied the animal's twitching black nose and gazed into his almost soulful eyes. "Nice to meet you, Phil." He then tipped his own imaginary top hat to the man carrying him and moved away to let those behind him get a little closer.

He leaned into Amy as they joined the buffet line. "You might have warned me."

"Sorry, I was having too much fun. Besides, it's your fault for not knowing who Punxsutawney Phil is."

He spooned some mac and cheese onto his plate then looked up to notice the woman with the camera he remembered from the first day. She was a little ahead of them in line, and he tapped Amy's arm to point her out.

Amy acknowledged with a nod, and after they'd filled their plates, they followed her, weaving a narrow trail between tightly packed tables. Amy found a seat next to the woman and Guy sat across from her, where he could also watch those still in line for any sign of the pickpocket in action. Amy was right. This crowded venue would also be a good place for the thief to ply his trade.

"Hi!" Amy said, getting the woman's attention. "We met yesterday. I hope you're enjoying Punxsutawney."

"Oh," the woman said, struggling to remove the camera strap around her neck. The strap had tangled in her hair.

"Let me help you with that." Amy assisted her with the camera then helped her remove her coat. "I'm Amy, by the way. And this is my friend, Guy."

"Brenda," she said. "Brenda Hall. Thanks for the heads-up on the B&B yesterday. Sorry if I didn't seem grateful. I guess I should have done my research before I came."

"I hope you're having fun regardless."

"Oh, I think it'll be worth it. It's just, I had so many things planned. I wanted to check out the B&B and the diner and jump in that puddle at the curb, you know."

Amy murmured consolingly. "Did you travel far to get here?"

"Almost seven hours from South Bend, Indiana," she said, then chuckled to herself. "Joke's on me. Would have taken less than half that to get to Woodstock. They now have a Groundhog Festival too." She held up her fork in a show of determination. "Next year."

"You must be quite a fan," Guy said, poking at his food. He couldn't identify the meat buried in heavy gravy. He hoped it wasn't groundhog.

Brenda sat up straighter. "I'm actually the head of the second largest fan site. And we're *this close*"—she pinched her thumb and index finger about a half inch apart—"to becoming the largest.

That's why I wanted to come, to get my own pictures. Sometimes those movie people make you take down the screenshots, so I wanted to get a bunch of my own to go along with a blog post of my trip."

"No wonder you were disappointed," Amy cooed. She really was good at this.

"Yeah, I still got tons of great pictures of all the statues in town. Well, most of them. I'm still missing three. And pictures of the bands and the artists and the vendors. And lots of crowd shots."

"You've been taking pictures of the crowds?" Guy asked.

"For sure," she said. "I've got a thousand of them so far. You know, sometimes celebrities sneak into these things, thinking nobody will recognize them with all the hats and gloves and stuff."

"Celebrities come to Groundhog Day?" Guy asked.

By now the table had filled up, and a man in a flannel shirt and baseball cap chimed in. "Sure. I saw Fred Rogers here back in the eighties."

"Really?" Brenda turned to him and snapped the man's picture.

While Brenda chatted with the newcomer, getting all the Mr. Rogers details, Guy nibbled at his food and stared at the camera on the table. While it looked old-fashioned at first sight, he could now see it was actually digital. She very well could have thousands of pictures on it.

When he looked up, he noticed Amy eyeing it too.

"You know, I would love to see your pictures," Amy said.

Brenda whipped out a homemade business card. "The best ones will be online shortly after Groundhog Day."

"Any chance of seeing all of them? And sooner?" She beamed that smile again. Guy didn't know about Brenda, but he would have coughed up the photos immediately.

"That would take hours," Brenda hedged. "I don't think—"

"Maybe you could copy them onto a thumb drive?" Amy suggested.

"Absolutely not!" Brenda started to rise out of her seat. "How do I know you wouldn't publish them yourself? Or worse, sell them to one of my competitor's sites?"

Guy leaned into the table. "I promise, we're not with any fan site. To be honest, I've never even seen the movie."

At that, Brenda's eyes widened, her jaw slacked, and she dropped back into her chair. "Never seen the..."

Guy shook his head. "I'm interested in the crowd shots, but not to hunt for any celebrities. A pickpocket took something valuable from me."

"And not just from him," Amy added. "Several other people as well. You might have photographic evidence of a crime taking place."

"Oh." Emotions buffeted Brenda's face. Would she part with her beloved photos to help a stranger?

"Let me think about it."

---

The Jackson Theater, housed in the Punxsutawney Area Community Center, was a mere block and a half north of Barclay Square, so after a brief crowd-watch in the park, Amy and Guy walked to the talent show. Quite a few people had already assembled at the free event when they arrived. Some wore costumes of various design, ready to parade their talents before the judges. Others moved immediately to the audience section to slouch in their seats and cheer—or jeer—them on.

Drawn by the irresistible aroma of popcorn, Amy followed her nose to the source and nabbed two bags before joining Guy, who'd staked out aisle seats midway to the front.

"Mmm. Thanks," he said. He continued to observe the crowd as they filed to their seats.

Amy glanced over the gathered audience too. A panel of judges sat near the front. More costumed performers sat in the audience on the far right, poised to go on stage when their turn came.

Guy leaned closer. "What about you, Amy? Do you have any hidden talents? Yodeling. Dart throwing. Sword swallowing?"

"I'm creative enough, I think, but I'm afraid my talent leans almost entirely to the textile arts. So unless the audience wants to wait around while I knit a sweater…"

"Nothing to put you in the limelight?"

"Well, I have done some spinning."

"Spinning? Like some kind of whirling dervish?"

Amy laughed at the thought. "Nothing quite so dizzying. I meant with a spinning wheel. But mainly for school classes and the historical society as a demonstration."

"In costume?"

"I *might* have made my own period-correct costume. Again, textile arts."

Guy squinted at her. "You're holding out on me. Come clean, now. What else do you do?"

"How do you know that?" Amy said indignantly. "Maybe you should be up on stage as a mind reader."

"So, there *is* a hidden talent."

"I sing. A little. Mainly in church."

"Any good?"

"Nobody's walked out of the service, but it doesn't mean I'm ready to go up on the big stage. What about you?"

Before he could answer, the house lights began to flicker, signifying the beginning of the show. Then the emcee began making introductions.

A group of about twenty cloggers, the women in colorful folk dresses and the men in lederhosen, mounted the stage first. Amy didn't know much about clogging, but their feet all seemed to hit the ground together, and the audience applauded their performance. Then again, if each member of the group brought along one or two family members, they'd have quite an advantage in that department.

A dog-training act led by two teen girls followed. Unfortunately, the dogs seemed preoccupied with the stage lights and the noise of the crowd and failed to cooperate with any of their commands. The audience applauded politely at the end, but then one of the dogs left a souvenir on the stage and a few couldn't help laughing.

"Poor things," Amy murmured.

There was a short break while volunteers cleaned up the stage, followed by a passable country singer with a slightly out-of-tune guitar.

When the applause for him died down, the emcee announced, "And here he is, Punxsutawney's own, Sparkleman!"

While the audience clapped, a magician, complete with tuxedo and a top hat, entered the stage. A sequined green vest and matching bow tie shimmered as they caught the houselights, probably the inspiration for the name Sparkleman.

Guy leaned forward in his seat and grabbed Amy's hand. "That's him. That's the magician from the park yesterday."

Guy was right about one thing. The magician wasn't particularly good. He did a handful of card tricks, of which only three succeeded. Then he reached into his hat.

Amy wasn't exactly sure what the magician had planned for his grand finale, but she suspected it didn't involve blood dripping from his fingers as he chased a rabbit off the stage, which is what happened.

A few in the audience clapped politely, some murmured a word of sympathy, but more laughed.

Guy rose from his seat. "I'd like to talk with him."

They propped their popcorn bags on the floor and left their coats draped over their chairs. Amy followed Guy to the rear of the auditorium, and then they cut up the right aisle and mounted the stairs to the backstage area.

By the time they arrived, Guy didn't see the magician anywhere. There was only a hunched-over volunteer wearing plastic gloves wiping up a trail of tiny blood drops with antiseptic wipes. The trail led to an external door.

Guy pushed it open and poked his head out. "He's there." He beckoned Amy to follow.

She stepped outside, holding the door open with her shoulder as she took in the scene. The magician had just managed to secure the unruly white rabbit into a crate, and then he shoved his fingers into his mouth. He was gaunt with a thin face, icy blue eyes, and blond, almost white, hair cropped short to his head. Amy estimated his age at twenty, if that.

"Stupid rabbit bit me," he said.

"You really should wash that," Amy said.

"You think?" he said, shaking his hand.

Amy nodded. "Go ahead. We can watch your stuff."

His stuff included the rabbit cage, the top hat, and two large duffel bags, probably containing more props. He hesitated a moment. But when Guy held the door open for him, he ducked inside.

Amy folded her arms tightly to her body in a vain attempt to preserve warmth as the chilly air tried to penetrate the open weave of her sweater and abscond with her body heat.

"Sorry," Guy said. "In the movies, a true gentleman would have a suit coat to drape around your shoulders." He tugged regretfully at his pullover. "Here." He drew a little closer, leaning his chest against her back while rubbing his palms up and down her arms. "Any better?"

One last shiver ran through her, but she did feel warmer. "Thanks."

He folded his arms in front of hers, his hands over her hands, and she leaned into his embrace. It felt so comfortable and natural that moments later she launched into full panic mode.

What was she doing? Sure, he seemed like a nice man, but that didn't mean she was ready for a romantic relationship. She'd worked too hard to get to a place of independence. She was a property owner. A businesswoman. She didn't need to lean on anyone.

She pulled away just as the magician pushed open the door. He now had several layers of paper toweling draped around his hand.

"That rascal got me good." He grimaced. "Tell me the truth. How bad was I?"

Amy swallowed hard, trying to think of a tactful answer. She looked up at Guy, and he returned her glance, his mouth open, but his lips not moving.

"You don't have to tell me." The magician kicked a small pebble across the sidewalk. "I knew that rabbit act wasn't ready. I practiced for weeks to do the disappearing cabinet, but my assistant couldn't get off work."

"That must be frustrating for you," Guy said.

"You're telling me," Sparkleman continued. "I'm trying to launch a business doing this. Don't get me wrong. I know I'm not ready for the Vegas Strip or anything, but I thought maybe children's parties, that kind of thing."

"Seems like the way to start," Amy said.

"Kids are a lot more sophisticated these days. I mean, I've done the card tricks, for like, forever. But they want to see the big illusions. And those things don't come cheap, even if you do build them yourself. The plans still cost money." He shook his head. "At least I hadn't rented a truck yet. I figured if I could win third place or higher, I could pay for it. Now I'm only out the cost of an Uber."

"Is that what you're waiting for?" Guy asked.

"We could drive you home," Amy said. "Although my car's a few blocks away. Where do you live?"

"Just over at the boardinghouse on Park, so it's not far. Nice of you, but I'm good."

"I'm Guy, by the way," Guy said. "This is my friend, Amy."

The magician didn't respond.

Amy tried again. "And what's your name, when you're not Sparkleman?"

"Oh," he said. "Uriah. Uriah Stutzman. Uri's good."

"I saw a few of your card tricks yesterday morning in the park," Guy said.

Uri scowled. "Don't talk about yesterday. It just adds insult to injury."

"Why?" Guy asked. "What happened?"

"The police, that's what happened. Do you know you need a license to be a street performer here? Officer threatened to bust me. I needed to either fork over a boatload of dough or 'cease and desist.' Well, I looked into the license. There's no way I could have earned my money back.

"And then they started asking me all kinds of questions about pickpocketing."

Amy held her breath and tried to keep her face casual.

"There *was* a pickpocket working the park," Guy said. "He got me."

"Really?" Uri said. "I thought the cop was giving me a hard time for the fun of it."

"So you didn't see anything suspicious?" Amy asked. "Someone working the crowds while they watched you perform?"

"Naw, didn't see anything like that."

Amy thought he answered a little too quickly. Then again, maybe he didn't want to be involved.

Guy's phone dinged. He pulled it out of his pocket and looked at the screen. "Just a second," he said, walking away.

"I should go." Uri jammed the top hat back onto his head, slung both duffel bags over his left shoulder, and then picked up the rabbit cage with his right hand. He nodded a curt goodbye, looking much like a well-dressed vagrant as he staggered down the sidewalk under the weight of his equipment.

"He left quick," Guy said as he shoved his phone back into his pocket.

"It's okay," Amy said. "I know where that boardinghouse is if we want to talk with him again. But tell me about the text. Good news, I hope. Your sister?"

"Not my sister," he said. "But I hope it's good news. Brenda Hall agreed to let us see her pictures."

# Chapter Six

Snow began to fall as Guy and Amy returned to Barclay Square, and by the time they arrived, had grown heavy enough to drive much of the crowd back to their homes and hotels. Instead of their planned people-watching, they drove to Panic.

"This is more than nuisance snow," Amy muttered as she peered through her windshield, her wipers slapping a slow rhythm.

"What's that?" Guy asked, stirring. Amy wondered if he'd fallen asleep.

"The snow," she repeated. "The weather guy called for 'nuisance snow.' This seems heavier than that."

"Should have asked me," he said.

A couple of inches covered the ground as she turned onto her property. Winnie and a few of the group-home residents were outside with shovels, and Amy waited until they were safely out of the drive before she swung her car into a spot in front of her shop.

Winnie waved them over.

"Do you need a hand?" Guy asked.

"No," Winnie said. "These guys like the work. Right, David?"

David said, "Right!" Then he saluted. "Hey, what's your name?" he said to Guy.

"Guy."

"No kidding?" David said.

"Kind of a silly name, huh?"

"It is," David said. "You're just some *guy* I know. Did you find the police station? Did they help you? The police officers are good helpers."

"The police are very good helpers, and they're trying."

"Good." And with that, he went back to shoveling.

Winnie turned to them with a grin. "Any luck in the great wallet hunt?"

"Maybe a little," Amy said. "We found a woman who took a bunch of pictures at the park yesterday morning. She's going to drop a thumb drive by later."

"And I might be able to gain access to my funds tomorrow, assuming everything checks out," Guy added. "It's hard enough to be homeless, much less penniless," he teased.

"How about a hot meal?" Winnie said. "Both of you. It's pasta night, and we've got plenty." She turned to Guy, "Although inviting an Italian over for pasta is a lot like trying to sell coal to Newcastle."

"Sure we're not imposing?" Amy asked.

Guy discreetly tapped her arm. "Pasta sounds great to me."

"Ah," Amy said. "Sounds good."

"Six?" Winnie said but didn't wait for a reply. One of her charges had slipped and fallen into a snowbank, and she rushed to give him a hand up.

Amy went to her car to retrieve her garment bag then unlocked the door to her shop. Cap'n Hook and Stitch, no longer shy of Guy and obviously hungry, came tearing out from their perches and started circling Amy's legs. "All right already. You'd think I never feed them." When she reached the base of the stairs, she turned and said, "You want a Coke or something?"

"Sure, that'd be great." Guy slipped off his coat and draped it over the chair at the table. Amy could see the fatigue on his face as he lowered himself gingerly into a seat. Maybe the snow that curtailed their plans was a godsend.

She went upstairs, hung up her dress, fed the cats, rinsed and refilled their water bowl, used the restroom, washed her hands, and then grabbed two Cokes from the fridge before heading back down to the shop.

She slipped one in front of Guy then took a nearby seat. "I don't know about you, but I'm exhausted. Kind of glad not to have to cook tonight, actually."

"And it gets us one step closer to a look at her wedding pictures," Guy said. "We'll just have to be alert for natural opportunities to bring up the topic."

Amy laughed. "So that's what you were after. I suspected you might be avoiding my cooking."

Guy looked hurt. "I don't know what you mean. After all, you made the best groundhog soup I've ever eaten."

"You think you'll recognize him from a photo? You said you didn't know him well."

"That kind of image never leaves you."

She studied his face. He stared out the window at the snow, but she wondered if those events weren't replaying in front of him. He shook his head, like a dog shakes off bathwater, then met her gaze. His brows furrowed. "Don't give me that look. It's not me you should feel sorry for. I made it out of there, at least."

"Yeah, but it must have been hard for you."

"Most of the following weeks were a blur. These things happen when you're unconscious. Then there's the pain meds. After that, it's just rising to the next challenge. Therapy. Physical therapy. Occupational therapy."

"It seems like you're doing well now."

"Well, I've never shirked a challenge."

"You sound like Winnie," Amy said. She drained the rest of her Coke. "She prefers to call her residents' issues 'challenges' rather than 'disabilities.'"

"There's wisdom there," Guy said. "Self-pity, that's the enemy, especially for a person of faith."

"How so?" Amy asked.

"It's easy to start doubting whether God is good, whether He's kind or loving, as if anything disturbing that comes into our lives is evidence that He's sleeping or doesn't care.

"But there's a reason for what He allows. We may not see it at the time. We may never truly understand it, but He's promised to be with us, in the green pastures and in the valley of the shadow. And I've had to learn to trust Him in both places."

Guy's gaze was intense, and she dropped hers to the tabletop.

He cleared his throat. "Anything I should know about the group-home residents before tonight? I mean, David I'm fairly sure has Down Syndrome, but I don't know anything about the others."

"If you're asking about diagnoses, I don't even know myself," Amy said. "I asked Winnie when they first moved in, but she sat me down and dictated terms."

Guy chuckled. "She set you straight?"

"Yes, she told me to let her worry about that. She said they already had plenty of doctors and social workers and therapists and counselors. What they really needed was a friend, and I should just treat them like everybody else."

"Sounds like she's in their corner. And they come here for classes?"

"Yeah, she got a grant to pay for them. Some are better than others at intricate work. Violet, she's the one in the wheelchair, has more physical challenges and needs more help, but she's also the most creative. They've managed to sell some of their work for pocket money."

"So, there's David and Violet…" Guy started numbering them on his fingers.

"There's Melanie," Amy said. "You didn't hear it from me, but I think David is sweet on her. Then there's Pete. Don't let him start telling silly riddles, or you'll be saying 'who's there' to his 'knock knocks' all night. And Kyle. Kyle doesn't talk much, but Winnie says he's pretty sharp, so I talk to him without expecting him to answer, and he seems to like it. I've caught him smiling a few times anyway.

"Which reminds me, Winnie said the guys' bathroom sink was dripping, so I'd better be a good landlord and get my tools."

"How'd that come about? The house too big for you?"

"You could say that," Amy said. "Actually, I never intended to live there."

He sent her a confused look, so she went on. "I dated this guy in college, an architecture major who grew up with a whole family that did construction, and his thing was flipping houses. Every spring he'd search for a property to renovate during the summer. Then he'd hire a bunch of college students to do the grunt work. It was kind of fun, actually. We'd all bring our sleeping bags, like indoor camping.

"I was a textile arts major, but he flattered me into thinking I could handle the design work, picking paint color and tile and flooring and stuff. I guess I did okay. And I learned a lot of skills. Before our senior year, he'd already bought one old farmhouse in Panic, then this one came on the market. He convinced me to drop my tuition money into it as a down payment and mortgage the rest."

"Uh-oh."

"Well, we flipped his first, and it sold like a shot. But by the time we finished this one, well, as they say, the market had taken a dip." She traced a small scratch on the surface of the table with her finger. "I thought," she said, without looking up, "that he'd share the proceeds from his sale to at least help me with my tuition. I mean, we'd been dating for two years, and I thought maybe he was *the one*, you know. But then he was like, 'Well, maybe you could get a loan.'

"I missed one registration deadline after another, then he went back to school and I stayed here, still trying to sell the place. Crickets. Mortgage payments started coming due, so I tried to advertise it as a vacation rental."

"And that didn't work?"

"It's hard to have a vacation rental when people only want to rent places around here one day a year and it's the same day. Otherwise, it was mostly guys wanting a place to crash while hunting and fishing, but half the time they'd trash the place."

"Ah."

"So I put it up as a long-term rental, right at the time Winnie was looking for a new group-home location. It covers the mortgage and then some. And I put my new flipping skills to work building the loft and shop."

"How's business going?" he asked.

"Better than it looks from the foot traffic," she said, laughing. "The grant with the group home helps a lot, and I do crazy internet sales on hand-dyed yarn. One of the fashion schools in New York must have put my link in their curriculum, because you wouldn't believe the orders I send to dormitories. But I get sales from all over. And a great deal on the raw yarn from some of the Amish women nearby."

"I didn't realize the Pennsylvania Amish came this far west," he said. "But it makes sense. There's Amish to the north too, in New York."

"The big tourist spots are all in Lancaster County." She tapped the table. "I should get those wrenches before it's too dark to see."

She moved to the area behind the counter, pulled her coat off the hook, and shrugged it on. Then she reached for the key ring she kept on a nearby hook, but it wasn't there. She found it on the floor where it must have fallen.

A gust sent a snow squall into her face as soon as she opened the door, and she turned her collar up then trotted over to the shed. She jammed the key into the cold padlock then blew on her fingers to warm them. Once inside, the shed provided protection from the wind, but the cold proved just as numbing. Using her cell phone flashlight to pierce the dimness, she found her small box of wrenches and other plumbing material then stopped. Something was off.

She took quick inventory. Nothing seemed to be missing. And everything was roughly in the same spot. Maybe Winnie had borrowed something and returned it. Maybe her imagination was running away with her.

She grabbed the box of plumbing material and set it outside while she secured the door and lock. She stopped for a moment to scan the horizon. Through the wavy farmhouse windows, she could see figures moving about in the kitchen, probably working together to prepare the pasta. A plow rumbled by, also spreading salt to help the remaining "nuisance snow" melt. And down the road at the vacant neighboring farmhouse, a light flickered in the window then winked out.

She blinked and looked again. Nothing but darkness and silence. Probably a headlight from the passing plow had hit the old farmhouse window. Or maybe her imagination *was* running away with her.

---

Guy followed Amy into the back hallway of the farmhouse, drawn by the familiar aroma of simmering tomato sauce. He watched, chagrined, as she kicked off her boots and left them on the mat. Instead of following suit, he leaned against the doorframe and diligently wiped all traces of snow onto the mat. He hoped that would suffice. They hung their coats on a rack just inside the door, on top of a mound of others of diverse sizes and hues.

Guy recognized the kitchen style as modern farmhouse, both from his sister's house and the home improvement shows that played on her television when he visited. Wooden floors, light gray Shaker-style cabinets, big caged-in pendant lights in black metal, and a huge island in the middle with a countertop that looked like marble. Here Melanie dumped bags of salad into a large bowl, and David stood next to her, shaking bottles of salad dressing. Beyond the island, the kitchen opened to the living room and dining room at the front of the house.

He could see why the table from Amy's shop no longer fit here, although a substantial table filled the dining room where Violet was already seated. A tall, thin, clean-shaven young man laid out silverware, his expression serious as he lined up each utensil.

"Come in, come in," Winnie called. "Don't offer to help. These guys take their work seriously."

"That's right," David said.

"You're our guest," Melanie added, and David smiled at her. Yup, Guy thought, David was smitten.

"Smells great in here," Amy said.

The tall man came into the kitchen with an extra fork.

"Hi, Kyle," Amy said. "This is my friend, Guy."

"Hi, Kyle," Guy said.

"Done with the table?" Winnie asked.

Kyle nodded with a half smile but didn't make eye contact.

"Why don't you pick out a spot at the table," Winnie said. "We pulled up an extra chair. Pete is working tonight and won't be home until later. We'll be ready for salad in a few minutes."

As they entered the dining room, Winnie introduced Guy to Violet. She had red, curly hair tied up in a messy bun, with wavy bangs brushed forward extending to her brows. She wore a peach sweater and a bright pink feather boa that she swished with her fingers as she talked. Her speech was slurred, and as they chatted, Guy listened as Amy, in her responses, often repeated what Violet had said, simultaneously verifying what she'd heard while translating for Guy, who was less familiar with her speech pattern.

The other residents filed in, taking up the remaining spots at the table. Eventually, Winnie stood behind the chair at the head and waited for a break in conversation. "Okay, I think we're ready. We usually start with a quiet moment. Some may wish to pray silently; others might choose to reflect on something good that happened today."

There was a rustle around the table as everyone reached out to hold the hands of those next to them. Kyle reached out to Guy on his left while Amy's hand slipped comfortably into his right. He smiled at her then looked up across the table just in time to see David and Melanie join hands with a similar smile shared between them. *Uh-oh.*

Guy bowed his head and thanked God for the food, asked for help in learning whether he'd found the right Winnie, asked for more help in locating the missing letter, then begged for the wisdom to understand his feelings for Amy.

When he raised his eyes, the others at the table had finished and a couple were staring at him.

"Let's eat," Winnie said.

Salad was served family style and accompanied by general, happy chatter. Most of the residents discussed the booth at the park and what they hoped to do with their money. An overnight trip to Pittsburgh seemed to be in the running.

"They put the fries right in the sammich," David said.

"It's messy," Melanie said. "But fun."

"Real fun," he said.

When everyone had finished their salads, Kyle, David, and Melanie carried the bowls back into the kitchen and returned with heaping plates of pasta. There was spaghetti with huge meatballs, fettuccini with Alfredo sauce, and some kind of ravioli to boot. Guy hadn't seen so much pasta since the family dinners at his grandparents' house. It sobered him a moment as he remembered the same congenial atmosphere around the dinner table, his grandparents and all the uncles and aunts and cousins, and often a guest or two. Through the years the faces disappeared. Some moved away, and others succumbed to illness, until all the family he could claim was his sister, and she had her own family. That thought caught in his throat, and he took a long sip of water to wash it down.

By the time he rejoined the conversation, Victoria was teasing Amy about not trying the meatballs.

"I have meatballs," Amy said.

"Where?"

"I like to hide my meatballs under my spaghetti, like buried treasure." Amy used her fork to push away the spaghetti, revealing two plump meatballs underneath.

This seemed to capture the attention of the table. David started burying his own meatballs.

"I have treasure too," Melanie said. "Real treasure. I have a whole box of treasures. Want to see?"

She started to get up, but Winnie convinced her to wait until after dinner.

Guy watched Amy during the rest of the meal and followed her lead in talking with the residents. She really was great with them, being the friend that Winnie had suggested, and Guy was taken with her cheerful banter. The conversation was simple and frank, lacking the usual filters and facades many people put up, and her face lit with genuine affection, not the soul-sucking sympathy that repulsed him. Long before dessert, his belly—and his heart—were full.

While the male residents cleaned up—as per the schedule on the refrigerator—the rest moved to the living room for coffee and cheesecake. Guy would have loved to squeeze in next to Amy on the sofa, but instead chose a higher wingback chair from which he could more gracefully extract himself.

"Can I get my treasure box now?" Melanie asked.

Winnie nodded, and Melanie ambled up the steps. A chairlift ran along one side of the wide staircase.

"I wonder what it is," Violet said. Already, Guy found it less difficult to understand her.

"I guess we'll find out what it is in a minute," Amy said.

Melanie started down the stairs carrying a large cardboard box that threatened to slip from her grasp.

Guy was glad he'd chosen the wingback. "Let me help." He rose quickly and stretched his arms over the banister to stabilize the box.

"Thank you! That was close!" Melanie said before setting the box down on the coffee table. Her "treasure box" was a bit beat up with lots of markings. Originally, it bore the logo of one of the larger publishing companies, then someone had written *LOST AND FOUND* in large capital letters with a thick black marker. This was crossed out in red marker, with *TREASURE* written underneath it.

"Where'd you get that?" Violet asked.

Melanie's smile lit up her whole face. "David gave it to me."

David entered from the kitchen, beaming.

Melanie opened the box. She pulled out three mismatched gloves, a Rubik's Cube, and a long multicolored scarf.

"Put it on," Victoria encouraged.

Melanie draped it around her shoulders and leaned close to Victoria, who still sported her pink feather boa.

"Just a second," Amy said, and took out her cell phone for a picture.

"David, where did the box come from?" Winnie asked gently.

"The library," he said.

Winnie leaned forward. When she finally spoke, her tone was even and calm. "Did you have permission to take the lost-and-found box from the library?"

David nodded. "They were going to throw it away. Said they'd hung on to it long enough."

Melanie continued to pull things from the box. There was a GED study guide, its pages marked with a scrap of sequined green fabric, a blue knit hat with a tattered yellow pom-pom at the top, an ancient calculator, a small ring that looked like it might have come from a gumball machine, and a tatty plush groundhog entangled in a mass of charging cables.

Violet pulled the scrap of fabric from the book and held it in the light. "Sparkly!"

"It is sparkly," Amy said. "You know, that might be as sparkly as Winnie's wedding dress. I've seen the photographs."

Winnie cast Amy a warning look, which she ignored.

"Oh, can we see?" Violet was apparently a fan of sparkly.

After a few mild protests and a withering look at Amy, Winnie left the room, returning a moment later with a fat white photo album.

The girls gathered around. While Melanie and Victoria oohed and aahed over the photographs, Amy looked on serenely, an almost cherubic expression on her face. At the next turn of the page, she beckoned him over with a quick tip of her head. While the first pictures in the album apparently focused on the bride and bridesmaids in all their finery, the current page showed the groom, clean-shaven and his hair slicked back, in a crisp suit with a single white rose boutonniere.

Guy held his breath as he let his eyes retrace the groom's features. The man in the photo was so young, so unaware of what the next intervening years would bring.

But there was no mistake. They'd found the right Winnie.

Now if he could only find the message.

## ∽ Chapter Seven ∾

Amy had resisted the impulse to ask more about Winnie's ex in front of the residents. After all, she'd heard the story and related most of it to Guy already. Sobering, though, to know for sure that somewhere out there were the last words her friend's ex had for her.

As much as she'd convinced herself that it was better to keep Winnie in the dark unless that mysterious envelope could be found, Amy found it a difficult confidence to keep. She shuddered at the possibility that she'd be left to keep the secret alone.

A plastic bag hung from the doorknob of Amy's shop when they returned, and she peeked inside to see a thumb drive. There was no note.

"Must be from Brenda," she said as they made their way back into the shop, the cats beginning their routine of circling her ankles. "Do you want to take a look at them now?" She checked the time on her fitness tracker. A little after nine, but she felt invigorated by what they'd learned.

"Like me to make a fire down here?" he suggested.

"Great! How about some hot cocoa too?" Amy didn't wait for an answer. The cats raced ahead of her up the stairs.

Amy came back downstairs about ten minutes later, a cozy cardigan draped over her shoulders and her laptop case slung over one arm. She carried a tray with two steaming mugs of cocoa and a bowl of buttery-smelling microwave popcorn.

Guy had made quick work of lighting a fire in the woodstove and was already seated on the sofa in front of it. Amy hadn't switched on all the overhead lights when they'd returned, and it made the fire's glow all the more vibrant. The crates of yarn that lined the walls were at one moment hidden in the dimness, but then the fire would spark and crackle, illuminating them, only to have them sink into darkness again.

She set the tray on the table, joined Guy on the sofa, and booted her laptop.

"Not sure I have room for popcorn after that big meal next door," Guy said, picking up a piece and eying it.

"This felt like homework, and that's my homework food," Amy said. "Besides, that's the benefit of popcorn. It kinda breaks down and fits in all the little leftover places in your stomach."

"Is that a fact?"

"I read it online. It must be true."

"Ah," Guy said, pulling out his cell phone. "Speaking of online, I got a text from Brenda, saying she dropped off the thumb drive and she's trusting us."

"Aw, that's good to know." She took a sip of cocoa.

"Then she says if any of her pics pop up online, she'll know it's us and she'll sue."

"I sense some trust issues there," Amy said. Her laptop sprang to life, and she inserted the thumb drive and found the picture files.

Guy scooted closer, and she balanced her laptop across both their knees. His shoulder touched hers as he leaned in to look at the screen. Okay, maybe this didn't feel exactly like homework.

"There." He pointed to a directory marked with yesterday's date.

Amy clicked on it. Was it just yesterday that Guy rolled into town?

She scrolled through the thumbnails, checking the time stamps and counting hundreds of pictures from yesterday morning alone. "Wow."

Guy grabbed a handful of popcorn. "Better get to work."

The first few dozen shots were of various buildings around town, probably Brenda's early attempts to identify locations from the movie, and Amy paged through them quickly. The first shot of Barclay Square was a selfie of Brenda and "Freedom Phil," a smiling groundhog statue painted in copper paint and decked out like the Statue of Liberty. In the background, various vendors set up their tents.

Here she slowed, as they'd need to take time to look at not only the focus of Brenda's pictures but anything happening in the background as well.

As they progressed through the morning's pictures, the crowds grew heavier, and Amy zoomed in several times. "We're looking for someone lurking about?"

Guy took a long breath. "We may also want to keep our eyes out for me and the other...*victims*." He shook his head. "I really hate that word. Kind of like *disabilities*."

"Criminally challenged?" Amy tried.

Guy laughed. "How about *pickpocketees*? Maybe we could see who was standing nearby."

Three pictures later, Amy spotted the family they'd seen at the police station. Brenda had renamed the picture "Jennifer Lawrence?"

Guy leaned toward the screen. "Can you blow that up?"

Amy zoomed in and tilted her head to study the picture. "I guess the mother looks a *little* like Jennifer Lawrence. If you changed the nose a bit. And the chin."

"And the eyes. And the brow line. And the hair color."

"And the kids." Amy laughed. "Yeah, I think Brenda is safe from us absconding with her celebrity photographs." She closed the picture and went back to the file list, where dozens of pictures were renamed after the celebrity. "She seems convinced though. Brenda was quite the stalker."

"Could work in our favor," Guy said.

Amy carefully studied the pictures of "Jennifaux," as Guy dubbed her. Brenda had photo-chronicled the woman's journey for almost an hour, by the timestamps. They saw pictures of Jennifaux and her family lined up at one of the food trucks then sipping hot beverages. They warmed themselves by the s'mores fire then watched the chain-saw artist before stopping for a selfie with the groundhog mascot. Brenda even took a shot of the poor woman ducking into a portable restroom with her young daughter.

The next shot showed Jennifaux and company taking in the street magician's act.

"I think we should talk to him again," Amy said. "Both you and another of the pickpocketees stopped to watch."

"Good idea," Guy said, squinting at the screen. "In fact, I think that's me there. May I?"

Amy relinquished control of the laptop, and Guy went through the next few pictures.

"Maybe we could talk to the other pickpocketees too," he said.

"Sounds like a good idea."

Cap'n Hook, who'd been curled up on the sofa, stretched out a tentative paw and yawned before climbing onto the warm spot on Amy's lap left by the laptop. Amy reached out and stroked the soft fur around his head and neck, and he started purring almost immediately.

Her neck had grown stiff from bending over the pictures, and her eyes felt dry and gritty, so she leaned back and closed her eyes, just for a moment.

---

Guy rubbed a kink out of his neck and looked up to see Amy asleep. The cat in her lap blinked, as if warning him against waking her up. He watched her for a moment. Yes, it had only been two days, but it had been an eventful two days that had thrown them together almost constantly, and he felt as if he'd known her much longer.

He closed the laptop and set it on the coffee table then gingerly rose from the sofa. He took one of the crocheted blankets—maybe she had made it herself—and tucked it around her, careful not to displace the cat, who still eyed him warily.

Time had reduced the fire to glowing embers, so he added a log. He washed up in the small half bath then looked around the shop, considering where he might sleep. The other end of the sofa seemed improper.

Instead, he gathered the rest of the blankets Amy had left him and prepared a makeshift bed next to the large table. He turned off more of the shop lights then used the pulled-out chairs as extra support to help lower himself to the floor.

Everything looked different from this vantage point in the soft light, and the shadows drew his attention to the underside of the table, near where the leg met the tabletop.

He ran his fingertips along what he first thought were scratches but then realized were more deliberate. He traced a line—no, an arrow—with his finger and then went to work deciphering the other scratches embedded into the grain. Letters, maybe initials. The second, he was pretty sure was a *W*. The first, maybe an *I* or a *T*. Possibly some maker's mark, a mystery of bygone years in Panic.

---

Amy woke with a start, not entirely sure what woke her. In the semi-darkness of the shop, she saw no sign of Guy. The cat had also deserted her, leaving one leg chilly while the other was warm and cozy under a blanket—a blanket she was certain hadn't been there when she'd dozed off.

She squinted at the time on her fitness tracker. Three a.m. Plenty of time to sleep in her own bed where she belonged.

Knowing the locations of all the creaks in the floor, she started a circuitous path toward the stairs. She found Guy stretched out on a pallet of blankets next to the table, snoring lightly, with Stitch on his chest.

Amy felt a pang of guilt for stealing her guest's slightly more comfortable perch but then consoled herself that he was probably used to far more primitive conditions.

Stitch stood up and stretched. Amy watched for a second, thinking that if Guy woke up, she could tell him she'd vacated the sofa. But he merely stirred then continued snoring as Stitch walked across his leg toward her.

While she was watching, Stitch's claw snagged in the blanket, and she started to drag it with her.

Amy rushed in, picked up the cat, and untangled her claw. But before she could drop the corner of the blanket back into place, she saw the prosthetic leg underneath. Guy had apparently removed it and put it next to him under the covers.

She gently lowered the blanket over him then crept upstairs.

Instead of finding her own bed as she'd intended, she dropped onto her sofa, cradling the cat close to her.

Guy's vague reference to his injury in the military, the limp, the long recovery—it all made sense now. As did his cagey answer when she'd asked him if he ran—and his reluctance to attend the Groundhog Ball.

She scratched Stitch between the ears. "I can't believe I asked him to polka." She shook her head and laughed at herself. "Why didn't he just tell me?"

That question kept sleep from her eyes, so she shifted into housework mode, feeding the cats, tidying her loft, and starting a load of laundry. She slid a fresh batch of muffins into the oven before showering and dressing.

When her coffee finished percolating, she texted Guy, not wanting to wake him or catch him without his prosthesis, at least until he felt comfortable sharing that with her. If he ever did.

A few moments later, the early morning hush was broken by the sound of his steps on the stairs. She could now detect the odd cadence to his steps and was surprised she hadn't noticed it before.

Amy poured hot coffee into colorful, chunky mugs, and they ate muffins seated at her small kitchen table. She did her best to hold up her end of the friendly banter but found it difficult. The prosthesis didn't bother her, but the great effort Guy had taken to conceal it from her did.

Eventually, the topic came around to plans for the day, and Amy rallied. "The only thing on my calendar is a demonstration this afternoon for the historical society."

"In costume?"

"I'm afraid so," she said. "Right in Barclay Square."

"I don't want to miss that," he said. "I also need to try the bank again, see if they've gotten everything approved."

Amy crossed her fingers. "And if you still want to talk to some of the…pickpocketees, we could drop by the B&B this morning. We know one family is staying there, and it's not far from here."

"We get to meet Jennifaux?" Guy feigned excitement, his eyes twinkling.

"And then there's the ball."

"Yeah, about that…"

"Don't try to wiggle out on me," Amy said. "It's still a great opportunity to keep an eye out for that thief, maybe schmooze a few people and see if we can learn anything." When Guy didn't respond, she added, "That's really why I want to go. I'll probably leave my dancing shoes at home."

If that was what was bothering Guy about attending the ball, he didn't acknowledge it, but he put up no further resistance either.

Their breakfast finished and their plans made, Amy went down to her shop. She checked her website and packed up a couple of orders that had come in. She ducked out without a coat to load them into her trunk and caught sight of Winnie at the farmhouse door.

Winnie waved her over. "Coffee?" she asked. "You look like you could use another cup."

Amy helped herself to a mug on the rack next to the coffee maker that served the residents. She popped in a pod claiming to be gingerbread flavored and took a sniff of the steam then a tentative sip before sprinkling in a little sugar. "Mmm, tastes like Christmas. Thanks, I needed that."

They pulled up stools next to the kitchen counter.

"What gives?" Winnie said. "You look glum. Everything going okay with your houseguest?"

Amy waved her question off then reconsidered. "I found out something unexpected about him last night, or rather, early this morning, and I don't know what to make of it."

Winnie remained quiet, sipping her own coffee.

Amy rushed to fill in the silence. "Guy's missing a leg."

"I thought that might be the case."

"You knew?" Amy's eyebrows shot up. "How?"

Winnie shrugged. "The limp, and then it caught my attention that he never took off his boots last night. At first, I thought it was a little rude, but everything else he did was polite. That, and he didn't sit next to you on the couch even though he looked like he wanted to."

Amy scratched her head. "You think so?"

"He's sweet on you. Guaranteed."

"I was beginning to think the same thing. A couple of times last the way he looked at me, I thought he might try to, you know, kiss ..." Amy felt her cheeks flush, and she avoided her friend's eyes. "But he didn't." She put her elbows on the counter and rested her chin on her folded hands. "Why the secrecy? He must think I'm really shallow."

"Maybe you're reading too much into that." Winnie pushed her aside. "After all, you've only known each other a few days. He might not be ready—"

"For a relationship, you mean? I can imagine, with all he must have been through..."

Winnie laughed. "Now you're reading into what *I* said. Settle down for a second and take a lecture from your friendly neighborhood social worker. If you think he backed off because somehow he's too broken, put that thought out of your mind. Honey, I've seen broken. Looks nothing like that. From what you've said and from what I've seen, it looks like his faith has sustained him through some very difficult circumstances.

"The residents here, they all have challenges too. Only thing is, they can't hide theirs very well. It doesn't take long for people they meet to realize something's 'off.' And then comes the reaction. Sometimes it's avoidance. Sometimes it's pity. No matter what else my guys and girls have to offer—joy, talent, humor, kindness—some people only see the disabilities."

"But that's not what *I'm* like," Amy said.

"I know that. And that's why you've been so good for the residents here. Besides knowing how to fix leaky faucets."

Amy smiled.

"I'm saying maybe Guy doesn't want his challenges to define him. Maybe he wants you to see the real him first, the man inside, and not lead the conversation with his physical challenges."

Amy took a sip of coffee then stared into her cup as she considered this.

"Or maybe," Winnie said, "he's using his independence to disguise the fact that he's scared of getting hurt." She cleared her throat. "Like *someone* I know."

---

Amy didn't speak much on the short drive to the bed-and-breakfast, and Guy didn't know what to make of it. They'd seemed to be getting on well the day before. He remembered stealing a glance at her while she'd pored over Brenda's pictures and thought how easy it would have been to sweep those errant waves of hair from her cheek, pull her closer to him, and kiss her.

He shook the daydream away. Today he picked up mixed feelings, both from her and from himself.

Maybe it would be better to put a little emotional distance between them. The time was all wrong for a romance. He still hadn't found work. Yes, he had that interview in Philadelphia, but there was no guarantee he'd get the job, especially with the delay in his arrival. Even if he did, the place was wrong. She seemed very attached to her home and life in Panic. And Philadelphia was 271.8 miles away. Yes, he'd googled it. As for the woman? Nothing wrong about her.

She flipped on her blinker, and Guy craned his neck to read the sign for Woodlands Bed-and-Breakfast.

The structure was similar to Amy's farmhouse but with an exterior employing more cedar and stone, giving it a mountain lodge vibe. A circular drive with extra parking had been installed in front, and in the center space a collection of cedar swings was clustered around a huge stone firepit.

"They've been able to make a go of a B&B here," Amy said. "They're a little closer to Punxsutawney and on a more traveled road. I know the owner, so it shouldn't be a problem just dropping in."

The oversized double doors opened onto a spacious lounge area, the ceiling high and covered in warm pine. Leather sofas in a putty color overlooked a floor-to-ceiling stone fireplace. A dining area in the rear was still arranged for breakfast, and the aromas of bacon and coffee hung in the air.

A middle-aged woman backed out of a side door, carrying a coffeepot. She set the pot down and brushed her hands on her apron before coming to greet them warmly.

After introductions—and declining the offer of yet another breakfast—Amy launched into what brought them there.

"The other day at the police station, I overheard some of your guests. I gather they ran into a pickpocket."

"You must mean the Simmons family. I felt bad when they told me what happened. Lovely family. Kids are a tiny bit rambunctious, but they're supposed to be at that age. I rather miss that, you know."

"Are they still here?" Guy asked.

"Guy also had his pocket picked that day," Amy explained.

"Did they take much?" the woman asked.

"Everything I had with me. But the worst part is they took something that didn't belong to me, something I was entrusted with, that I'd really like to get back."

"We thought," Amy said, "that maybe if we talk to some of the others, we could figure out a common link. Maybe something they all did or someone they bumped into."

"You're in luck. They're still here, booked for the full Groundhog Day experience. They usually come down for breakfast right around now, so if you'd care to wait…"

Guy and Amy took seats in the living room in front of the fireplace, and Guy's gaze swept the room. He could see why guests would choose this place. It struck a familiar chord too, with its wide plank floors. Rustic but cheery.

"Amy? The other house you helped decorate, the one your ex-boyfriend flipped…we're sitting in it, aren't we?"

Amy took in a long breath. "Yes. The new owners thought the space would make a delightful bed-and-breakfast."

"If it bothers you being here, we don't have to stay."

Amy waved him off. "I'm okay with the location. Now if *he* were here, that might be different. Although I guess everything worked out like it was supposed to."

"But your last year of college—"

"I managed to finish remotely. It just took a little longer. And I was pushed to be on my own and open my business a little earlier than my comfort zone allowed for. It was scary at the time, but now—my business, Winnie's friendship, the group home—I can't imagine a better outcome."

The sounds of little feet galloping down the stairs interrupted them, and soon the parents were helping the Simmons kids fill their plates and settle in at the table. Guy and Amy gave them a few minutes then headed over to join them.

"Mr. Simmons?" Guy asked.

"Yes?" Mr. Simmons was a square-faced man wearing glasses a little bit too large for his face, giving him a quizzical expression.

"I hear we have something in common," Guy said. "Someone stole my wallet in the park the other day."

Mr. Simmons blew out an exasperated breath. "Wasn't that the weirdest thing? Fortunately, my wife had hers and a bit of cash. Otherwise, we would have been up a creek."

"Tell me about it," Guy said. "If not for Amy here, I'd be sleeping in my car."

"He's staying in my shop," Amy added quickly, and Guy realized she meant to keep them from any wrong conclusions.

"The thief also took something else," Guy said. "A message I was entrusted with, and it's rather important to get it back."

"How can we help?" asked Mrs. Simmons.

"Maybe if we put our heads together," Amy said, "we might come up with somebody you all had contact with. Someone you bumped into or someone lurking about. Maybe even a distraction."

"Wow," the man said. "Kind of a blur to me now." He turned to his wife. "Do you remember anything?"

She shrugged while cutting a pancake into bites for one of her children. She passed it to the youngest boy then licked syrup from her thumb. "We stopped several times. I remember a magician."

"He was awful, Mom," her older son said. "Didn't even let me keep the quarter."

"Why should he let you keep the quarter?" his sister asked.

"Well, it came out of my ear. Why shouldn't I keep it?"

Guy nudged Amy. "See, I told you."

"Eww!" said the girl. "Ear wax money."

"Enough of that. Eat your breakfast." Mrs. Simmons shook her head. "I don't remember much else in particular, but I have a few pictures on my phone, if that might help."

"That would be great," Amy said. She leaned over to put her number in the woman's phone. Amy's phone began dinging as the images came in.

"I hope you find what you're looking for," Mr. Simmons said.

Once they climbed back in the car, Amy pulled a wet wipe from her purse and cleaned syrup from her fingers and some from her cell phone. "Perils of dealing with kids," she said, laughing. "Everything sticky. Fries and Cheerios on the back seat."

"Sounds wonderful," Guy said.

Amy held her phone between them, and they started looking at the pictures. She flipped through a bunch with the kids in front of various groundhog statuary and the kids eating, before coming across shots of the kids and the magician, the kids watching the chain-saw artist, the kids dancing the polka under the watchful eye of a smiling accordion player. And two attempts at the same selfie with the groundhog mascot.

Amy stared at it without comment, but looked up at Guy, her mouth open with the question she seemed hesitant to ask.

"Could it be the groundhog?" he asked.

# Chapter Eight

Amy shook her head. "I can't imagine the organizers would put anyone into that suit who wasn't fully vetted. Groundhog Day is too important to them, to this town, and being the mascot is kind of an honor." She paused, still looking at the picture, but its large round eyes, smiling face, and buck teeth didn't provide any new information. "Do you remember running into the mascot that morning?"

"I remember seeing him," Guy said. "He was all over the place at once. You know how those things are." He stared at the picture. "Maybe we should talk to someone at the police station. They could check into it."

Amy rubbed away a sudden headache. "They're so busy. I'd hate to steer them in the wrong direction on nothing more than a hunch. How about this? I'll look for one of the organizers and ask who's wearing the suit this year."

She started the car, waited for the windows to defog, and then they headed back to Punxsutawney.

She managed to find a close spot on the street. She always dreaded parallel parking but tried it to save Guy a few steps. After several attempts, Guy directed her through the last one, and she slid the car perfectly to the curb.

"You are a woman of many talents," he said.

She laughed. "Parallel parking isn't one of them."

They walked the short distance to the park, and Amy made a beeline to the first empty bench they found.

"Tired?" Guy asked. "Don't you want to walk around and look for one of the organizers? You'd recognize them before I would."

"I thought you might want to...well, I mean, we've been on our feet a lot the past few days."

Guy dropped onto the bench next to her and stared out at the crowd. "What gave me away?"

Her shoulders sank. "The cat. Stitch pulled your blanket off early this morning."

"Should have named her 'snitch' then."

Amy took in a deep breath then exhaled slowly. "Why didn't you tell me?"

"Does it matter?"

"Only that you didn't tell me. I hope you don't think I'm that shallow that it would make a difference."

He shook his head. "Has nothing to do with you. It's not something I tell anyone if I can help it. It seems to work out better that way, to keep some distance."

Amy didn't respond. She blinked back a tear but didn't have a clue why.

"My ex-fiancée," he said. "Lucinda. We were engaged, and she showed up at Walter Reed shortly after I did."

"She left you because of the leg?"

Guy shook his head. "No, it's because she didn't leave me. She showed up. She helped. She brought magazines and a sorry-looking plant. She fluffed my pillows and insisted on calling down when they messed up my food tray. She even played cheerleader with my therapy, pushed me to keep going."

"I don't understand."

"The longer she did it, the harder it was on her. She wasn't my fiancée anymore. She became my caregiver, and she had too much character to tell me it was draining the love and life right out of her. *I* broke it off. She deserved better."

"You seem to be doing okay now."

"It took a long time, but I learned to compensate, to function independently."

"So that's all you want out of life, to function independently?"

"I don't want to be a burden on anyone, especially someone I care about."

"But to allow that fear to keep you from getting close to people…"

"Isn't that what you want too? Independence? You don't want to get hurt any more than I do, am I right?"

"I'm doing okay."

"Me too. So what are we arguing about? Why do you care?"

Amy stewed over their discussion but didn't say anything more, instead concentrating on getting her heart rate back under control. Why *did* she care?

As she stared out at the milling people, she noticed a top hat sticking above the heads of the crowd. She rose and headed in that direction, weaving her way through the densely packed park.

"Hey, where are you going?" Guy called out.

Amy pushed on. When she caught up with the top hat, she recognized the wearer as one of the Inner Circle, the event organizers. She tapped him on the arm and stood in front of him, trying to catch her breath in the cold.

"Could I ask..." Plans to subtly bring up the topic failed her. "Who's wearing the groundhog costume this year?"

---

Guy sat on the bench and watched the pom-pom on the top of Amy's hat disappear into the sea of winter wear, like the sails of a boat sinking below the horizon. He considered letting her disappear, become a footnote of a bad weekend in Pennsylvania.

But he couldn't let her go like that. He'd been unnecessarily rude, abrupt, and self-centered. He must have allowed his attraction to show, encouraging her to reciprocate his feelings, even while he'd congratulated himself on how cleverly he'd disguised them. He'd shunned relationships to avoid hurting someone he cared about, and the practice had led him to do that very thing.

He pushed himself up and started to follow but found himself swallowed up by a park full of strangers talking, dancing, eating. Even among so many, he was alone, and deep down he knew he had himself to blame for that.

He spun in a circle, scanning the crowd for the sight of her. He found the booth for the group home, thinking that she might seek out Winnie, but a couple of the residents were staffing the booth along with an aide. He checked the lines at the food truck and scanned the benches by the firepit.

Maybe he'd gone too far. Surely she'd come looking for him, so he retraced his steps. An elderly couple now occupied the bench, huddled close together while they shared a hot pretzel.

This was silly. Why was he running after her? They'd spent the last couple of days in forced proximity. If she needed space, she could have as much as she wanted.

He turned up his collar at a sudden chill and set his feet in motion toward the bank.

---

Amy had recognized the tall, top-hatted organizer from a photograph in the newspaper. What she hadn't noticed when she'd run up to him and blurted out her question were the other, shorter, top-hatted men surrounding him, embroiled in a discussion.

He held up a hand to her, as if asking her to wait, and she stammered out an apology before dropping to the background.

She tried not to eavesdrop but gathered they were discussing a problem with the fireworks display planned for the next day at Gobbler's Knob. When they had reached some kind of consensus, the man turned to Amy but then looked at his watch.

"Walk with me?" he said.

"Sure," Amy said, although the man hadn't waited for a reply before taking off at a brisk pace. She almost had to trot to keep up with him.

"So what's this about?" he asked.

"Have you heard about the pickpocket?"

He stopped abruptly. "Terrible thing. Terrible thing. Not something we want to be known for. We brought on more plainclothes security, and we think we can nip it in the bud. Soon."

Amy looked around but couldn't see any increased security.

The man laughed. "If you could recognize the plainclothes security then we wouldn't be getting our money's worth, would we?" He adopted a sympathetic expression. "Are you one of the victims?"

"Not me," she said. "A friend of mine." She turned to look at the bench, but Guy was no longer there. "He's around here somewhere."

"Not sure what I can do to help. I suggest your friend go to the station and file a report."

"We already did that. My friend lost something valuable, and we've been trying to recover it."

"I don't follow you."

"We talked to several others who were targeted that morning, and we've been looking for commonalities."

"So, *that's* why you want to talk with the chief of police."

"I…no. I didn't say anything about talking to the chief. I'm not sure we know enough to bother him yet."

"We're talking about two different things, aren't we?" he said.

"I think so. All I really want to know is who's wearing the groundhog costume this year. See, the groundhog keeps showing up in all the pictures."

"And you're thinking the *groundhog* is somehow involved in the thefts." He gave her a strained smile. "Your theory might just need a little bit of work. But now I understand how we got confused."

"Why's that?"

"The person wearing the groundhog costume this year *is* the chief of police."

## Chapter Nine

Guy left the bank with a new ATM card and a few hundred dollars in cash, which he distributed to several different pockets. They'd even allowed him to use their computer to print out a temporary driver's license from New York's DMV website. He then ducked into a neighboring drugstore and found a replacement wallet. Once his permanent license and credit cards arrived at his home address, it would be like nothing had ever happened.

Only it had, and he felt little relief at recovering this aspect of his life.

He took a moment to send one last text to his sister, to add to the mountain of those he'd already sent, letting her know he no longer needed her financial assistance. He then began a text to Amy to tell her he now had access to his car and money. He began a follow-up text, struggling to find the right words to apologize for his manner earlier.

While he composed the text, an email popped up asking for confirmation of his postponed interview in Philadelphia, and he confirmed then slid his phone into his pocket.

Now the clock was ticking. Soon he would be on his way, whether he recovered the missing letter or not. He glanced at the time displayed on the drugstore sign then used his phone's mapping system to plot a route to the boardinghouse on Park Avenue where the magician was staying. It wasn't far from his current location, so he decided to walk.

The groundhog or the magician? Those two figures seemed to crop up in everyone's memory, but there was no proof either was involved. If he spoke to both, might he suggest a trade? The letter for his silence?

That idea carried the aroma of extortion and didn't sit well with him at all.

He hadn't finished formulating questions to ask when the boardinghouse came into view. The house was spacious but not grand, old but not historic. Any charm the exterior ever had was plastered over with gray vinyl siding. Chipping paint dripped from exposed trim, and the foundation needed repointing, at the very least. One elaborate arched window near the top of the gable may have been its last remaining original feature, but now it had a certain horror movie–poster vibe to it.

He climbed the crumbling steps, mindful of the slanted roof above him, and knocked.

A gaunt, sallow woman with a head full of tight gray curls answered the door. She would have been almost gargantuan in height if she hadn't been hunched over a too-short walker. She wore a dingy beige sweatsuit with cartoon characters on the top, now mostly washed off. The pants were too short, revealing white athletic socks.

"Looking for a room?" she asked in a deep, throaty voice that suggested she was or had been a long-time smoker.

"Actually," Guy said, "I'm looking for a roomer of yours. Uriah, the magician."

A tea kettle whistled behind her. "You'd better come in then."

She shuffled down a narrow hall of textured and yellowed paint, which may have once been eggshell white, and he followed her into a small eat-in kitchen. She gestured to a fifties-era chrome-and-Formica table, but he remained standing, in part from politeness and in part because a huge orange tabby was curled up and asleep on the proffered chair.

She slid a cup in front of him without asking then shooed the cat away. She plopped down onto the other chair, with accompanying relieved sound effects. "So, it's Uriah you want to know about."

"Actually, I wanted to talk with him." Guy took a tentative sip of his tea, so weak it was hard to distinguish from hot water. "Is he at home?"

She let out a bark of laughter, revealing a mouthful of silver fillings. "Well, he might be home, but he certainly isn't here."

Guy squinted at her.

"He might be home," she said, "but he's not here, because here isn't home for him. Not anymore, that is."

"He's moved out?" Suspicious.

"About a year ago. I hate to lose a good tenant, and despite my misgivings, he was a good tenant. But when the girl showed up, I told him this was no place for a young lady." She reached over to a cracked and dusty cookie jar and lifted the lid. "Cookie?"

Guy declined, but she pulled one out for herself.

"So he had a girl living with him?"

"Not *with* him. I have a one-person-per-room policy, not that anything went on between them. He claimed she was his sister, and I didn't see anything to make me doubt that. She had that just-off-the-farm look about her, much like he did when he first showed up."

"They came from a farm?"

"How do you say you know Uriah?" She peered over her teacup at him. "Seems odd you don't know he was Amish. He came here during what they call *rumspringa*, you know what that is?"

"It's like a coming-of-age thing, isn't it?"

"It really means 'running around.' Although it's not usually all that wild like some of them reality TV shows say. Most of 'em don't stray all that far from home. They sow a few wild oats and then join the church.

"Uriah was a little different. I gather his home wasn't all that good. He never explained all the ins and outs, but he skedaddled out of there as quick as he could, determined to make himself a life away from his father. Of course, the Amish only go to school up to the eighth grade, so he didn't have that many options, you see. He went through a series of minimum wage jobs, and what he couldn't pay in rent, he made up in chores. Handy, he was. I kind of miss having him around."

"Where did the magician thing come from?"

"Saw his act, did you?" The woman rolled her eyes. "If I had a quarter for every quarter he pulled out of my ear, I'd be residing over in one of those fancy schmancy B&Bs and not this old house. I honestly don't know where it came from, but he did tricks from the moment he arrived, watching magicians on TV and sending away for things in the mail whenever he saved up a few bucks. I guess it was his get-rich scheme, his ticket to easy street. I think the only folks making any money were the ones sending him all them doodads, but he wouldn't hear it from me.

"I'd tell him, 'Save up. Get an education.' But that must have seemed like too much work for him. 'One more trick,' he'd say. 'One more trick and I can start doing parties.' In his mind, he was always one trick away from hitting the big time."

"And then his sister arrived."

"And then there were two of them. I would have been happy to keep them here, but a rooming house…some of the guys I get, I wouldn't want my sister around them, much less a seventeen-year-old who hasn't seen that much of the world. And with two of them and double the rent, they weren't making it. Eventually, I asked them to go."

"And they went."

"Felt bad about it. I figured they'd gone home. But if you say you saw his act, they must have found somewhere to live. I sure don't have a forwarding address."

---

Guy's stomach now protested the lack of lunch, and he checked the map on his phone. He'd skip over the fast-food strip he'd passed the other day in favor of one of the food trucks in the park.

His route took him down a few streets that were new to him, and as he traversed the sidewalk, he found himself approaching another of the smiling groundhog statues scattered around Punxsutawney. At first, he thought the caped figure was meant to represent a magician, but on closer inspection, the hat suggested he was more of a wizard. When he stood in front of it, he saw a weather vane mounted on the hat, and a working thermometer in his hand. A plaque underneath identified him as the Wizard of Weather.

Guy groaned. Weather wasn't magic; it was science. Why didn't anybody around here get that? But as he looked beyond the smiling statuary to the brick edifice behind him, he made out a sign bearing the words PUNXSUTAWNEY WEATHER DISCOVERY CENTER mounted under the original sign designating the building as a post office.

He ignored the rumblings in his stomach, gingerly climbed the stairs, and went inside.

---

Amy waited as long as she could at the park. She had wandered among the finished ice sculptures and even managed to score a bowl of winning chili from the cook-off, which she ate by the fire. Her historically accurate costume proved not quite as warm as her coat, hat, and boots had been.

Guy had teased her about wanting to see her spinning demonstration for the historical society, but he'd never shown up. She checked her phone, but there was nothing from him except his earlier text about now having access to his car—followed by her smiling emoji response, which seemed insufficient, given their last conversation before separating. As did HEADING BACK, which she sent now. She'd rather discuss the rest face-to-face. She scanned the park for him one more time then walked to her car. She considered driving over to the strip mall where Guy's car had been parked since his arrival but decided not to. She didn't know how she'd feel if he'd left town as soon as he had access to gas money.

The sky loomed gray and dismal as she wound those same country roads back to Panic. She turned on her headlights and flipped on the radio to wake herself up, realizing she hadn't done so since Guy's arrival. None of the stations interested her, so she switched it off and settled for the sound of her tires *shooshing* on wet pavement. When she pulled in, her car was the only one there.

When she flipped the shop lights on, she realized Guy's stuff was still there, so he must be coming back. She went straight up to her loft, fed the cats, and then took her dress out of the closet.

Where was he?

*If he didn't want to go to the ball, he should have said so*, Amy reasoned while she toweled off after a brief shower. But as she confronted her face in the foggy mirror, she realized he had said so, and more than once.

"You pushed him," she told her reflection. "You pushed him into a situation he wasn't comfortable with, and now you wonder why he stood you up?"

As she exited the bathroom, engine noise lured her to the window, but she saw only Winnie's van returning with several of her residents. They slammed the van doors and talked and laughed together as they entered the house and shut the door behind them.

She finished her hair and makeup then sat on the sofa for a few moments stroking Cap'n Hook's head and watching the clock. Finally, after another peek out the window, she shrugged on her coat and grabbed the extra key to her shop out of the junk drawer. She wrote a quick note on the sticky pad she kept on the entry table by her door then locked up, sticking the note to the outside door.

She walked over to the farmhouse.

"Ooh, that's the dress?" Winnie said when she answered the door. "Come in and show it to me."

Amy stepped into the kitchen, removed her coat, and did the prerequisite twirl.

"Has Guy seen it yet?" Winnie asked.

"I actually don't know where he is. He has cash and transportation of his own now, and I haven't seen him since."

Her words must have betrayed more emotion than she'd intended, because Winnie's brows drew together in sympathy, and Amy had trouble meeting her friend's eyes. She pulled the key out of her pocket. "Here. I left him a note in case he comes back for his stuff."

"I thought he was going to the ball with you."

"I thought so too, but…"

"Men." Winnie wrinkled her nose. "Look, I'm not making excuses or anything, but maybe he got tied up at the bank or lost track of time. Why don't you give me his ticket, just in case he's running late."

"I don't think—"

"What else are you planning to do with it?" Winnie said, holding out her hand.

Amy reached into her small clutch bag and handed it over.

There was still no sign of cars as Amy drove away, but she swerved to avoid the flickering bicycle headlight on the wrong side of the road. Her own headlights caught the face of the rider.

Olivia? Amy hoped the young woman wasn't headed her way for a class, but she'd made doubly sure all the groups knew classes were canceled until after the holidays. She pulled over to the shoulder but then watched as the bicycle continued past her driveway and kept going down the road.

Amy checked for traffic she already knew wasn't there and headed back to Punxsutawney.

---

Guy had driven five minutes on the wrong road before he realized he'd missed the turnoff for Amy's place in the dark. He'd been so confident he could find it on his own, but now he stopped on the shoulder and put the address into his phone, checking the time before shoving the phone in his pocket.

He hadn't realized it was quite that late, but he could dress in five minutes, and he had so much to tell Amy on the way to the ball.

Her little Civic wasn't there when he arrived, and his headlights lit up a pink sticky note on her door. He tore it off then trotted over to the farmhouse to collect the key.

Winnie answered his knock. "Look what the cat dragged in."

"I know I'm a little late. Amy said she left a key."

Winnie reached into her pocket and pulled out the key but kept her fist clasped around it. "Before I give you this, you and I need to have a little conversation. About Amy."

Something in her tone suggested this would be a rather one-sided conversation, so Guy stuffed his hands into his pockets and readied himself.

"Here's the deal. Amy is a special person. She's talented, open, and friendly."

"She really is wonderful."

Winnie glared at him, and he made a mental note not to interrupt again.

"It took a while to get her back to that place. Her ex-boyfriend really hurt her, just as she was beginning to trust him. But now she's more confident, more independent. She's accomplished so many things she set out to do and a few things she only dreamed about."

"What are you saying?"

"Don't get me wrong. I like you. But a word to the wise: Don't mess it up. Don't hurt her."

"That's the last thing I want to do."

"Then we understand each other." She tossed him the key. "Oh, and she told me to give you this, in case you were leaving." She handed him the ticket then closed the door.

Guy let himself into Amy's shop and sank down onto a chair at the table.

*Don't mess it up. Don't hurt her.*

Easier said than done.

He looked at her shop, a testament to all she had accomplished. And right next door were her friends, part of a life she'd established. A life that was perfectly complete and satisfying to her before he arrived.

He had no place here, certainly nothing to offer that would improve things for her. The intensity with which his heart ached at the thought of leaving her surprised him, considering how recently they'd met. But better sooner than later.

Instead of dressing, he retrieved his toiletries from the bathroom and stuffed them into his bag. He could be halfway to Philadelphia before Amy returned from the ball. He was about to throw his suit bag over his shoulder when he stopped.

He was being a coward. Winnie had said not to hurt her. Running out without a word would accomplish that too. No, he'd go to the ball, he'd thank her for her hospitality, repay her for her kindness—or at least for the trouble and expense he caused her—and they'd part as friends.

He made his way back to the sofa, where he could more easily slip into his suit pants. He buttoned his shirt on the way to the bathroom and tied his tie in the mirror. He shoved the ball ticket into his pocket then gathered his suitcases and stowed them in his trunk. He'd say his goodbyes at the ball and hit the road immediately afterward. He turned back to lock the door and stared into the shop.

That was when he caught movement in the window's reflection.

# ~ Chapter Ten ~

The shed door opened, and someone crept out. It was too dim to make out any details, especially since the intruder wore dark clothing and a dark ski mask.

"Hey!" Guy called out.

The intruder started running, heading toward the fields.

Guy followed. Just enough moonlight illuminated the snow-covered ground to see the figure moving like a shadow across it. This was not a speed race. The intruder's legs sank into the deep snow with each step. Guy reckoned his stride was longer, because he began to catch up. As he drew close, he reached out to grab a fistful of coat.

With the next step, his prosthetic sank into a rut, and his grasp on the coat pitched him forward. He fell on his face in the field.

The intruder fell too, but regained his footing quickly and scurried off into the night.

Guy pushed himself into a sitting position. His hand lighted on a thin, flat piece of wood, maybe four inches by two inches. It wasn't anything he recognized, but it felt too smooth to be natural. Maybe something the intruder dropped? He shoved it into his pocket to examine later.

He shivered, sitting in the snow wearing only his suit. He pulled his prosthetic leg in front of him and examined the connection. Everything seemed in place. He rolled over on his good leg then to his knees. He maneuvered until he was able to regain his standing position. Once stable, he took out his cell phone and used the flashlight to evaluate the best path back.

He let himself back in the shop, stopping on the mat to brush as much snow as he could from his suit, now damp in places and sporting a few patches of mud. So much for making a good impression.

He went to the bathroom and cleaned up as best he could, washing out a small cut on his forehead. He straightened his askew tie then locked up again and headed out.

---

The Groundhog Ball was an annual tradition, but the theme varied from year to year. This year, the attire, music, and decorations were more speakeasy than formal ball, and Al Capone would have felt more at home there than any fairy-tale princess or debutante.

The third time Amy caught herself watching the door, she bypassed the busy bar and chose a soft drink from one of the tables set up nearby. She took a sip and paused to listen to the jazz ensemble decked out in silver sequined jackets and black bow ties. A saxophonist completed an elaborate solo before sitting with the rest of the group.

The event photographer was engrossed in taking pictures of the band. He held a modern camera but wore roaring twenties' garb, complete with a press pass tucked into the band of his hat.

A young man wearing a wrinkled shirt, satin vest, and bow tie swooped in beside Amy. "Care to dance?" When she declined, he said, "Buy you a drink?"

"No, but thank you." Seeking a spot out of the line of bachelor fire, she headed toward the small tables set up on the perimeter. There, in the dimmer light, she recognized the honeymooning couple from the police station.

If they'd been alone, gazing into each other's eyes, she wouldn't have bothered them, but others shared their table. She adjusted her shawl, strolled over, and asked if the chair next to them was vacant.

"Hi, I'm Amy," she said, settling in and offering her hand to the woman.

"Jackie," she said over a mouthful of appetizer. "This is my... husband, Frank." She beamed in his direction. "Just getting used to introducing him that way!"

The couple across the table introduced themselves as Vince and Debbie.

Once Jackie had taken a sip of her drink, she said, "You look familiar."

Amy nodded. "I was at the police station the same time you were."

"Don't tell me they got you too?" Debbie said from across the table.

Amy's eyebrows rose. "Not me, but my friend." She gestured to Vince and Debbie. "You too?"

"We were just talking about it." Debbie said. "Craziest thing."

"When did it happen to you?" Amy asked.

Frank looked sheepish. "Must have been some time yesterday morning. I went to pay for lunch at the diner, and no wallet."

"Good thing I had my purse," Debbie said. "But it was the day before yesterday."

Frank thought for a moment, "Yeah, that's right."

"Same as us," Jackie said.

"What were you doing before you went to lunch?" Amy asked.

"Why?" Frank asked. "Are you with the police?"

Amy shook her head. "I don't mean to be nosy. My friend lost something valuable, well, more like sentimental. Something that actually belonged to another friend of mine but probably wouldn't be of any value to the pickpocket. We're hoping to get it back."

"Good luck with that," Jackie said. "The police told us the thief probably took the cash and dumped everything else."

"They told us that too," Amy said. "My friend's been poking through more than his share of trash."

"That's rough," said Debbie.

"We've been talking to some of the people who were in the park that morning," Amy said, "and looking at any pictures they'd taken. We haven't exactly caught the thief in action, but it feels like we're getting a better handle on a few of the same faces that keep popping up."

"I gotcha," Debbie said, already pulling out her phone.

"I really appreciate this," Amy said, "considering I'm a stranger to you."

"Hey," Vince said, "no strangers here. Only new friends." He held up his drink, and they all clinked their assortment of beverages over the table just as a flash went off.

"Now smile!" said the event photographer Amy had seen earlier.

He took another picture then tipped his hat.

"I thought you were here to take pictures of the band," Amy said.

The photographer groaned. "That took forever. Those stupid sequined coats kept catching the light. I must have taken dozens to get one that worked." He took another picture then tipped his hat again and moved on.

By the time Amy's vision had cleared, Jackie had slid her phone in front of her. Some of her photos seemed familiar, probably because Brenda had taken similar shots. The magician. The groundhog. Brenda.

"Yeah, I wondered about *her*," Jackie said, pointing to her phone. "Caught her taking my picture."

"We checked her out," Amy said. "She's taking pictures for her blog and likes to get lots of crowd shots, hoping for a celebrity sighting."

"I have pictures too." Debbie pushed her phone across the table, and Amy leaned in to look.

Vince and Debbie had apparently used the early morning hours to stalk the large groundhog statuary all around town. Amy counted eighteen selfies with smiling groundhogs in various costumes before coming to the one dressed as the Statue of Liberty, marking their entrance into Barclay Square.

Here Amy slowed, pausing a few times to zoom into areas in the background. There was also a blurry selfie with the groundhog, which Amy knew was just coincidental. She couldn't believe the chief of police could be the pickpocket.

"I'm sad that one didn't turn out," Debbie said. "I think we had the same problem the photographer just mentioned—the sun hit the sequins in his bow tie."

"Could be," Amy said. She was so engrossed in the pictures that when a hand landed on her shoulder, she jumped.

Guy leaned down. "Sorry I'm late."

She thought of a number of witty but slightly pointed rejoinders, none of which she wanted to air in public. She remained silent as Guy introduced himself to the rest of the table.

"Vince and Frank also had their wallets taken," she said. "They've been kind to let me see their photographs from the same morning." Only then did she look at Guy. "What happened to your face?"

"Long story. I'll fill you in later." Guy took a chair from a nearby table and sat next to Amy. "Learn anything?"

"I'm almost through looking at these," she said.

"More of the groundhog," Guy said, leaning over her shoulder.

"Wait, you think it's the guy in the suit?" Vince asked.

Amy sucked her lower lip. "I doubt it. I have it on the best authority that the mascot was fully vetted."

"Fully?" Guy asked.

"Above reproach." Amy stared at him, trying to telepathically send him a message to drop the topic. No sense in starting unfounded rumors.

"Are we back to the magician?" Guy asked.

Amy turned to Vince and Debbie. "What about you? Did you go anywhere near the magician that morning?"

"We saw him," Vince said. "But we didn't get close to him. We went back to catch his act, but by then the police were rousting him out of the park."

Guy leaned close as Amy looked through the rest of Debbie's photos.

"If there's something there," Amy said, "I don't see it." She returned the phone to Debbie. "Thanks anyway."

Guy spoke in Amy's ear. "I have to talk to you, but not here." He held out his hand. "Care to dance?"

---

By the time they reached the dance floor, Guy could have sworn the temperature in the room had risen twenty degrees.

Dancing hadn't been part of his occupational therapy, and he wasn't quite sure how to manage it. Before climbing out of his car, he'd done a quick online search looking for tips. The results included hundreds of videos of amputees participating in various forms of dance, including a truly graceful ballet dancer with a prosthetic leg and another with no arms. If they could do that, he reasoned, certainly he could fake the old sway-in-place technique to a slow song for a few minutes.

That confidence had fled, but he took Amy in his arms anyway and swayed to the cadence of the music.

"Is that where you went this morning," Guy asked, "to find out who was in the groundhog suit? I lost you in the crowd."

"Did you? I saw one of the Inner Circle, you know, the guys in the top hats, and I asked him."

"And?"

"It was the chief of police."

"The chief of police was the guy in the top hat?"

"No, the chief of police is wearing the groundhog suit this year."

*in Panic, Pennsylvania*

"Oh." Guy stopped momentarily. The music changed, and he had to adapt his swaying to a more vigorous tempo.

"So, what happened to you?" Amy asked. "I began to think you stood me up."

"I came close." He briefly recapped his day, starting with the productive visit to the bank and the unproductive visit to the boardinghouse.

"So, the great Sparkleman gave a false address," Amy said. "That could be significant."

"Could be a lot of good reasons he didn't tell us where he lived," Guy said.

She swept her fingers lightly near the cut on his forehead. "You never did tell me where you got this."

"Oh, that." He cleared his throat. "Those are merely the chivalrous scars I obtained while protecting your honor."

"My honor?"

"Well, actually, your shed." He related the story of the intruder.

"That's odd. I thought something seemed different in my shed, but it was locked up tight and nothing was taken. I thought maybe Winnie or one of the residents borrowed something."

"I couldn't see much of the intruder, but he was pretty agile and didn't want to be seen." Guy reached into his pocket and pulled out the small wooden object he found. "And I think he dropped this."

The music ended and the dancers applauded.

Amy took the object and led Guy to a better lit area by the coatroom. She held it in her palm. "This seems familiar." She traced a finger along the edges. "There's adhesive of some kind here. Still tacky, like it's part of something that someone tried to glue together."

"Maybe that's what they were doing in your shed," Guy said. "I wonder if the rest of it is still in that field. Along with what's left of my dignity."

"Wow, *my* honor and *your* dignity. A lot of important things at risk tonight."

Amy was joking, but the thought gave Guy pause. Did the intruder have anything to do with their search for his missing wallet? Because if he'd put her at risk in any way, he'd never forgive himself.

No way he could leave tonight, not if there might still be a menacing intruder nearby.

"It might be worth searching that field tomorrow," Amy said.

"That sounds like a lot of work," Guy said. "It's a big field."

Amy tilted her head and smiled. "I might have a few friends who could help."

---

When the first light came on in the farmhouse kitchen, Amy darted across the parking area and tapped lightly on the door. Winnie said she could scrounge up a few volunteers for a search and she'd bring them out by nine thirty.

"Come hungry," Amy said, then went back to her place and started baking. By nine thirty, she had a tray of muffins, fresh fruit, and hearty biscuit sandwiches filled with eggs, cheese, and bacon.

She'd been avoiding Guy, moving through the shop without engaging him in any meaningful conversation. Things had been comfortable enough at the dance the night before, but after they returned, she'd heard a trunk slam and had looked out the window just as he hauled his luggage back into the shop.

She'd assumed he'd been late to the ball because of his busy afternoon and the altercation by her shed, but the luggage in the trunk was evidence he *had* been planning to leave. Maybe he wasn't kidding when he'd said he almost stood her up. Even though he'd apparently delayed his departure, he'd have to hit the road eventually. And she knew she couldn't invest her affection in another person who was just going to leave. She needed to guard her heart. The more emotional distance she could put between them now, the less it would hurt later.

She carried the tray downstairs to the farmhouse table then went back up to her loft to gather her winter gear and the fresh pot of coffee she'd made for the troops. When she returned, Melanie and David had seated themselves at the table and Pete was already busy telling his jokes to Guy. Kyle stood near them, head bowed but wearing his shy smile.

Winnie came in the door a moment later, pushing Victoria. "Full crew today. Everyone wanted to help!"

They took time for breakfast around the big farmhouse table, and Amy breathed in the congenial atmosphere.

Finishing early, David and Pete began a friendly hockey game across the table using a crumpled napkin as the puck.

Winnie intercepted it. "Amy, why don't you tell everyone what we're looking for."

Amy held up the wood piece. "Last night, someone broke into my shed, and as they ran away, they dropped this. It's sticky on one side, so I think they'd tried to glue it to something. We want to search the fields to see if they dropped anything else. It may not look like this, but if you see anything besides an old cornstalk or a rock, grab it."

"Got it?" Winnie asked.

"Got it!" a few of them shouted.

Amy went over to Victoria. "Maybe you and Guy can look through the shed and the parking area to see if they dropped anything there."

"Looking for clues," Violet said. "Like Scooby Doo!"

"Then I must be Shaggy," Guy said leaning over her chair. "Ready?"

They took a few moments to put their winter gear on, Amy and Winnie making sure those with dexterity issues managed to zip their coats and fasten their boots, and then they headed out to the fields.

Amy owned the side field, but she rented it to a farmer who grew corn for animal feed. After the mechanized harvesting, only the short, tough stalks poked through the snow.

Amy's gaze followed Guy as he guided Victoria to the shed. She was glad she'd thought of a job for them to do. Victoria always seemed sad when she couldn't help like the others, and it was a good excuse to keep Guy off the uneven ground as well.

Amy could see the tracks in the snow that headed toward the field. She followed them to a spot where the snow was packed down and the stalks were broken or bent. "Over here, guys. Let's look over here!"

When she got closer, she took in the exact spot where Guy had fallen, making an imperfect snow angel. From there, a single set of tracks continued on, so she sent Winnie, Melanie, and David to follow them. Meanwhile, she kept Pete and Kyle to search the spot where Guy had caught up with the intruder and found the first piece.

"Should we look under the snow?" Pete asked.

"Well, it didn't snow last night," Amy said, "but something may have fallen by one of the cornstalks or got pushed under where the footprints are. So it couldn't hurt to look under there."

"Under the footprints," Pete sang. "Underfoot. My mama always told me not to get underfoot." He laughed at his own joke.

Kyle just smiled.

They'd searched for about fifteen minutes when Victoria shouted, "Found something! We found a clue!"

Amy told Pete and Kyle to keep looking while she headed back to the shed.

"It was right there," Victoria said, pointing to the spot where the lawn ended and the field began.

"It looks just like the other one," Guy said, holding it up. "It even has a sticky side too."

Amy pulled the first find out of her coat pocket and examined both together. Each was a thin piece of wood about two inches by four inches. Each had traces of glue along one of the long sides. She pushed them together, and a shiver ran up her spine. She closed her eyes. "I know what they are now."

"What?" Guy said.

She held them up in front of her mouth. "They're groundhog teeth."

"Groundhogs aren't that big," Victoria said.

"The one we're after is," Guy said.

# Chapter Eleven

Guy felt grateful to drive Amy back into Punxsutawney in his rental. Not that Amy was a bad driver, but she'd been forced to cart him around long enough.

"This whole thing has my stomach in knots," she said. "We can't accuse the chief of police."

"We're not accusing the chief of anything," Guy said. "We're simply going to ask how the investigation is progressing. Then we'll present what we've found and see how he reacts."

Amy massaged her forehead as if trying to rub away a headache. "I still don't see how it all fits."

"Let's start with what we know about the groundhog," Guy said. "The groundhog mascot seems to be the only common denominator the pickpocketees share."

"That we've seen, *and* that people remember."

"Right."

"We also know the person wearing the groundhog suit is the chief of police." Amy covered her mouth with her hands. "It can't be him," she mumbled through her fingers.

"Does seem like a long shot," Guy said.

"And why was someone in *my* shed?" Amy asked.

"We should probably report that too."

"Wrong jurisdiction," Amy said. "Panic is outside of Punxsutawney."

"Then who would you report to?"

"I'm not exactly sure," Amy said. "I've never had reason to call the police."

"What would you do in an emergency?"

"Dial 911 and let them figure it out."

Guy chuckled. "Makes sense."

"I don't get the motive," Amy said. "Why would the thief mess around in my shed? Assuming the two are related, which I still don't know how we'd prove."

"We've been asking a lot of questions. Maybe the thief got wind of it and decided to come out to your place to warn us off."

"By waiting in my shed? How did he even get in? The lock wasn't damaged."

"A magician might be able to pick a lock," Guy said. "Some of them are escape artists."

"So now we're back to the magician?" she asked. "Then why the groundhog teeth?"

Guy shook his head. "We probably still have a lot more questions than answers, but let's try talking to the chief. Couldn't hurt, could it?"

"Unless he's the thief. Which he's not, so it's okay. Right?"

His rental car didn't have a handicap plate, so Guy bypassed those reserved parking spots and kept driving, finding a spot to parallel park halfway down the block from the station. They passed the smiling groundhog police officer statue in front, which Guy found a little amusing, now that he knew the police chief had donned the suit.

Once inside, Guy saw an officer behind the front desk talking with the clerk.

"Can I help you?" the officer asked.

Guy explained who he was and asked to see the chief of police.

"If it's just a progress report you're looking for, I can tell you that we haven't generated any new leads. Sorry to say that."

"And I'm sorry to hear that," Guy said. "But I'd still like to see the chief, if he's in."

The clerk snickered. "I'm afraid he's not."

"He's…donning his other uniform today," the officer said.

"The groundhog suit?" Amy asked.

"You know about the groundhog suit?" the officer asked. "Don't tell him *we* told you. He's a little bit touchy about it. You know, the whole commanding presence doesn't really jibe with the cute, furry rodent suit."

"Do you know where he is?" Guy asked.

"Over at the park."

---

Guy turned up his collar against the cold as they walked into a rather stiff breeze on the way to the park. "Prevailing westerlies."

"All I know at this point is that I'd welcome an early spring this year," Amy said. "I wonder if the groundhog will see his shadow."

"I'm just hoping we'll see him," Guy said as they entered the park. He stopped to scan the crowd, letting his gaze sweep the food trucks and along the various merchant tents. He finally spotted the playful groundhog mascot cavorting with tourists not far from the ice sculptures. He pointed. "There."

A short line of families waited to take selfies with the mascot. Amy shrugged then she and Guy joined the queue.

"This is like accusing Santa at Christmas," Amy said.

"Remember, we're not accusing him of anything. Just asking him questions."

"Okay, then this is like questioning Santa at Christmas."

The line moved forward, and Amy and Guy stepped up

Guy craned his neck. "Well, he has his own teeth."

"Of course he has his teeth," Amy said. "The chief wouldn't pick your pocket, and he surely wouldn't break into my shed."

"I was just...gathering evidence."

The line moved up again, and it was their turn.

Guy took his phone out to take a picture, and the groundhog stretched his arms around each of their shoulders, pulling them closer.

Her lips half frozen in a smile, Amy said, "Chief?"

Guy snapped a picture. "We'd like to talk with you about the pickpocket."

They all leaned in for another picture.

"Can't talk here," the chief whispered. "How about the Burrow at noon?"

"The Burrow?" Guy asked, as he and Amy walked away. "As in where the groundhog lives? Wait, he must be joking." He turned around to head back to where the chief now frolicked with several children, their parents taking pictures.

Amy grabbed his hand. "It's not a joke," she said, leading him away. "It's a pub just outside the park." She stopped to look at the time on her fitness tracker. "Only twenty minutes until noon, so we ought to head there now if we're going to score a table."

They traversed the park and, before they even crossed the street, Guy could smell the fryers going full steam. Despite the pub's nondescript appearance, Amy wasn't wrong about its popularity. The line for a table extended to the door, and they made it inside only because people in front of them squeezed more tightly together. The next to arrive would be waiting in the cold.

The right side of the building boasted a huge U-shaped bar with a gleaming dark top and lighted coolers behind it. Every stool was filled—and some spilling over—with patrons eating, drinking, and ignoring the big screen televisions overhead. The left side was jammed with tables—four-tops, Guy remembered from a brief restaurant job in high school. Even if the volume of the televisions had been turned up, nobody would have heard them over the din of the full capacity crowd, amplified by the wood ceiling and concrete floors.

Guy hazarded a glance at the food on a nearby table. Tall, stacked burgers and hearty sandwiches, served in those red plastic baskets with an assortment of fried accompaniments. The air was redolent with vinegary hot sauces, fried onions, and the unmistakable aroma of beef sizzling on a hot grill.

His mouth watered. Definitely *not* too early for lunch.

The wait for the table took less time than he'd thought, and they'd barely draped their coats over the backs of their chairs before the server approached. They ordered soft drinks, and Guy splurged on appetizers to share: onion straws and the hot-pepper cheeseballs, which he had never had before, but they sounded interesting.

The chief, still in full groundhog gear, showed up just after the appetizers arrived. Many of those in the pub called out a greeting.

He waved to them then went straight back to the men's room. He emerged minutes later in street clothes, carrying a duffel bag. He spoke to the server on the way to the table then pulled out a chair and sank into it. "I should get hazard pay for that. Just sayin'. Those kids are something else. Thanks for meeting me here. Couldn't talk in the suit. I'm not supposed to break the *mystique*." He wrapped the last word in air quotes.

The server brought over a soft drink for the chief then took their lunch orders. Guy decided to try their Burrow Burger with a side order of house-cut fries. Amy selected a fish sandwich, and the chief asked for the special.

"So," the chief said, leaning on the table, "what did you want to talk about?"

Guy took a moment to introduce themselves and said he was one of the victims.

"I can see where you'd be curious," the chief said. "But I don't have much to tell you. Unless we catch him in the act or with stolen property—and we haven't—we have nothing to go on. We've been watching the park, and nothing has turned up. There haven't been any new reports since that afternoon, so he might have already skedaddled to some other town."

Guy looked at Amy and shrugged.

Amy pulled out the groundhog teeth and set them on the table.

"Whatcha got there?" the chief asked.

"We wanted to ask you that," Guy said. "Do they look familiar?"

"Oh, I don't know..." He cocked his head. "Actually, when you put them together like that, it kinda looks like the groundhog teeth to my costume." He scooted back from the table, reached down, and pulled the duffel into his lap. He unzipped it, exposing the mascot head on top, and held the teeth up next to the costume to compare. "Pretty close match. Where did you get them?"

Guy explained about the break-in of Amy's shed and finding the teeth in the field.

"That's a new level of weird," the chief said. "But I don't see how that connects with your pickpocket."

"That's just it," Amy said. "We've been talking to some of the others who were targeted, seeing if they remember anybody, and we've combed through a lot of pictures from that morning. And…" She looked nervously at Guy.

"And the one common denominator we've found was you."

"Me?"

"Yeah," Guy continued. "They all had close contact and took selfies with the groundhog."

The chief stared at him for a moment then started laughing. "I hope you're not trying to apply for a job as an investigator or anything, because if you're calling me a pickpocketing shed thief, you really missed the mark."

"We're not saying you did anything," Amy said. "We're just trying to figure out how all these things connect. Did you notice anything unusual in the park that morning?"

"First of all, that costume doesn't exactly afford a full field of vision. Second, I wasn't even in the park the day the pickpockets were reported."

"But we have pictures—" Amy pulled out her cell phone and started searching.

He leaned his arms on the table. "Wasn't me."

"Could someone have borrowed the costume?" Guy asked. "Where was it that morning?"

"Locked in my office at the station, giving all my guys a golden opportunity to mock me openly, which they did. So, no, nobody borrowed it." He grimaced and then stretched his neck. "There was another costume though. An old one. The Inner Circle paid to have a new one made this year."

"Yes, we talked to the tailor," Guy said. "There was no pattern, so they had to rip apart the old one and use that as a pattern."

Amy pulled up one of Brenda's pictures of the groundhog on the day of the thefts and held it up. "It certainly looks like the same costume." She set the cell phone on the table. "Only then he wore the bow tie."

"What bow tie?" the chief asked. "I never had a bow tie."

Amy and Guy simultaneously leaned in to examine the photograph of the mascot.

Guy cocked his head. "He's wearing a bow tie."

"A shiny, sequined, green bow tie," Amy added.

"I think I know *who* the thief is," Guy said.

Amy sat back in her chair. "And *I* know where to find her."

## Chapter Twelve

Amy turned up the car's heater and held her hands over the vents. Once the sun had set, the cold had seeped in quickly.

"We could go back and wait for the police to call," Guy said.

Amy shook her head. "We've come this far. I want to see it through." She used her scarf to wipe another viewing portal in the fogged-up windshield as they sat on her road, facing the neighboring vacant farmhouse. The area in between them held several official police vehicles. The officers had fanned out, some to the front door and some headed around the building. The chief must have put enough stock into their theory to pull this joint effort together.

"I can't believe we didn't notice the bow tie," Amy said. "That gave it all away."

"Because it showed there were two suits," Guy said. "I get that part. Instead of destroying the old one after using it as a pattern, that tailor's assistant—"

"Olivia," Amy offered.

"Olivia sewed it back together."

"Except the neck was probably damaged from how the suit had been cut apart, so she added the bow tie."

"But how could she pick pockets with groundhog paws on her hands?" Guy asked.

Amy thought for a moment. "She could have sewed a slit into the paw so she could get her hand out when she wanted to."

"So, *she* was our thieving groundhog," Guy said. "And here I thought it was the magician because he'd be good at sleight of hand."

"But so would a magician's assistant," Amy said. "Who also sewed the magician's vest and tie out of the same green sequined material."

"Ah, so Olivia was Sparkleman's missing assistant, who was also his sister, right?"

Amy nodded. "Two ex-Amish siblings trying to make a go of it outside their old community. She left a scrap of the material as a bookmark in that GED study book that Melanie got from the library's lost-and-found box. At one point Olivia must have wanted to further her education."

"She couldn't have been earning much working in that small tailor's shop. It's a bleak life plan for a young woman."

"Prospects are bleak for both of them. Uriah has dreams of becoming a famous magician, or at least a paid one. But even there, he doesn't have the resources to get started."

"Like he said, illusions are expensive, even if you make them yourself," Guy said. "And he's supposedly handy, according to his former landlord. But you also need tools for that. Which brings us back to your shed."

"Olivia came to classes. She must have spotted the key, taken it, and made a copy."

"And what's the deal on this vacant farmhouse again?"

"The owner still lived there when I moved in," Amy said. "Nice guy, but he was eighty-seven and a bit of a hoarder. Okay, more than a bit. When I realized how bad it was, I managed to locate his son, and they moved him to assisted living. Last I heard, he's happy there." She turned to Guy. "Lots more women than men, so he's very popular."

"Gotcha."

"I hoped someone would come and clean out the house before the rodents took over, but I guess it was too much work."

"So they just left it?" Guy asked.

"I thought I saw a light in the window the other day. But then I figured it was my imagination or a reflection."

"I get it. They're trespassing. That's how the police put together a warrant so quickly."

"They're trespassing, so they didn't need one," Amy said. "Just permission of the owner, or in this case his son, who was happy to give the police a key."

Guy took a sip of his coffee and put it back into the car's cupholder. "What's taking so long?"

Amy cleared the fog covering her window again. The police had set up high-powered lights that illuminated the property as if it were day. Amy looked at the sad house. Once it had held happy families. Now it sat neglected and unwanted, its roofline bowed and the paint nearly peeled off.

An officer waved a car through the road lined with official vehicles. In the changing light, Amy noticed shadows moving by the overgrown shrubs on the side of the house. She blinked hard and looked again. "Guy, they wouldn't have forgotten to watch the BILCO doors, would they?"

"What doors?"

"The door that leads from outside into the old cellar."

The shadows moved again, and this time Amy could make out two figures, low to the ground, creeping across the overgrown yard.

She opened her door and took off running toward a police officer. "Hey, over there!"

---

While Amy ran, shouting to gain the attention of the officer, Guy pushed his car door open and crossed the street to get a better look. He didn't think he could keep up with the fleeing siblings in the snow, but maybe he could help guide the officers in their pursuit if he kept them in sight.

"They're getting away!" he called out, and then he entered the snow-covered field.

It was slow slogging, carefully placing one foot after the other. He came across a fallen tree branch serviceable as a walking stick, and that gave him more stability. He continued on. Left foot, right foot. Before he knew it, he had gained on the thieves, who, in their haste, had fallen several times.

"Over here!" he called again to the officers. He could hear them closing in behind him.

"Stop!" Guy called out. He was now just ten feet or so from Uri and his sister. Their features were visible only by moonlight and the contrast of their dark clothing with the white of the snow.

Uri turned to him and stopped, lifting his hands into the air like some angel trying to take flight. Then he brought them both down, and a cloud of smoke appeared in front of him.

Guy held back, looking for Uri to reappear as the smoke cleared, but he didn't see either of them. By this time, the officers caught up and ran through the remaining fog.

Guy stood in place, feeling slightly defeated but mainly miffed. He should have figured a magician would try to make a grand attempt to disappear in a cloud of smoke.

Yet he'd been so close. If the two got away now, his chances of getting that letter back would be close to nil.

"Got him!" an officer yelled.

"There's two of them!" Guy shouted.

Then he heard Olivia squeal, and another voice said, "Got her."

Guy stood there in the field for a moment and closed his eyes, breathing in the chilly air and thanking God that the thieves were finally caught.

He only hoped they hadn't destroyed Winnie's letter.

***

One dim light shone in the farmhouse when they finally returned, and Amy tapped lightly on the glass. She and Guy waited as she heard Winnie make her way to the door.

"Ready for this?" Amy asked as she ran a hand along his back for encouragement.

Guy looked down at the letter in his hand and nodded. After he'd explained to the chief what the envelope held, Guy was a little surprised how quickly it had been returned to him. Apparently, the old farmhouse had yielded a wealth of other evidence.

"Come in," Winnie said softly. "Everyone was excited about all the police cars, but they finally settled for the night. You'll have to come over and tell them all about it tomorrow." She squinted at the clock. "Or make that later today. I sort of promised you would."

"We will," Guy said. "But we need to talk with you."

"Something serious?" Winnie's gaze darted from Guy to Amy then back to Guy again.

"Yes," Amy said. "Maybe we should put on some tea."

They shared tea and cookies while sitting around the island in the dim and quiet kitchen. Guy and Amy started first by telling the story of how they'd tracked down the thieves and how police had found the missing wallets under the bed Olivia used in the vacant house.

"Squatting right next door," Winnie said. "And her brother didn't know she was stealing?"

"That's the way they both told it," Guy said. "She was grateful to her brother for taking her in and wanted to help him become a great magician. She just told him she earned the money by doing extra work at the shop, and he didn't ask too many questions. He's not guiltless though. He knew they were illegally squatting there."

"Couldn't have done too much damage, the condition that house was in," Winnie said.

"I caught a glimpse of it," Amy said. "Frankly, it looked a lot better. They'd cleared out a lot of the junk to make it habitable. Threw out old food, ate whatever was still good. Any of the junk that was burnable went up in smoke in the fireplace to give them heat. They had water from the old well, had set up cages and coops in the barn for the rabbit and doves they'd sent away for. They even fixed the old bicycles that had been sitting around for decades and used them to get around. Everything they needed."

"No electricity, no lights."

"But remember, they grew up that way," Amy said. "I gather life with their father was even tougher. Even though they're both legal adults, they've had little preparation for life outside the community. I hope that gets considered when they go to trial."

"So they're pressing charges then?" Winnie asked.

"Have to," Guy said. "I doubt the charges against Uri will amount to much, but Olivia stole a lot of money and credit cards." He sighed and lifted the envelope and put it on the counter in front of Winnie. "And other things."

"What's this?" Winnie looked at her name on the envelope but didn't touch it.

"It's a letter I was asked to deliver," Guy said, "but it was stolen along with my wallet. It's the one thing I most wanted to get back. It's from—"

"I know who it's from," Winnie said, folding her arms. Amy didn't know if her friend felt cold or was putting up a wall. "How did you get it?"

Guy took a deep breath and related the story of his driver writing one last letter and asking him to deliver it. "I'm sorry it took a while to get here. I was injured myself, and…" He stopped, and Amy understood why.

Winnie had pushed her elbows onto the counter and was rubbing her temples, staring at the envelope. They remained silent while minutes ticked away. Finally, she looked up. "It's a lot to take in."

"You didn't know he had died?" Guy asked.

Winnie shook her head. "I haven't heard anything from him since the day he took off. I didn't even know he joined up."

"I wish I could tell you more," Guy said. "I only met him that last day."

She looked up at him through gleaming eyes. "You went to a lot of trouble for a guy you didn't really know."

Amy reached across the counter and put her hand on top of Winnie's. "And for you."

"He probably didn't list you as his spouse on his entry forms," Guy said. "If he had, the military would have contacted you directly. Still, if you never divorced, you're likely entitled to surviving-spouse benefits."

Winnie looked down at the envelope again but took a long while before moving.

Amy sipped her cold tea and watched as Winnie finally used a finger and traced along the outline of the key on the envelope then let her fingers rest on that single drop of blood. Just when Amy thought nothing would happen, Winnie sighed and ripped open the envelope. At the same time a floodgate opened, and her tears started dropping on the letter inside.

Amy grabbed several napkins from the stack on the counter and handed them to her.

Winnie shook her head. "Just when I thought that man had no more effect on me." Her voice cracked on the last words. She handed the letter to Amy. "Here, you read it. I can barely make out the words with all this silly crying."

"Not silly," Amy said, taking the letter. "Are you sure?"

Winnie nodded.

Amy read.

Dear Winnie,

    This letter is long overdue, and I'm sorry about that. I'm sorry about a lot of things, but if I only got a little time, I want to make sure you hear that from me.

    I was young and scared and stupid. That's no excuse. You were young too, but you couldn't run from cancer. Truth was, we still should be cuddling on some beach, but there I was watching your hair fall out, so weak you couldn't get out of bed. Every moment seeing you like that was torture.

    I got scared. Scared I couldn't take care of you, scared I'd lose you. And I ran. It didn't take long before I was ashamed of what I'd done, and then I was too scared to come home.

    I have no right to ask you to forgive such a coward. Things were hard, and I'm sure I just made them harder, but I wanted you to have this key. I couldn't bring myself to sell any of the things I took from you. I put them all in a safe-deposit box in Punxsutawney. You shouldn't have any problem getting them, being my spouse and all.

    All my love,
    Alan

Winnie pinched her eyes shut. "Thank you." She reached out and took the key and tightened her fist around it.

---

The night was still dark, the air clear and cold, when they finally left the farmhouse kitchen, but Guy heard rumbling in the distance. "That can't be thunder."

"Score one for the meteorologist," Amy said. "It's the fireworks from Gobbler's Knob. It's an all-night party until Phil finally wakes up." She pulled her coat tighter around herself and scanned the horizon. "It's hard to see the fireworks from here because of the trees."

They stopped and stared at the horizon anyway. Another faint rumble sounded, but no light showed.

"It's sad, really," Guy said. "I mean Winnie and Alan. He was too afraid to tell her how he felt until it was too late."

Amy sighed.

"I don't want to do the same thing. Amy—" He laid his hand on her arm.

"Guy, don't. I'll admit, I have feelings for you too, but it's pointless. The thieves are in jail, you delivered your letter, and that means you'll be leaving."

"What if I don't have to leave?"

"I thought you had an interview in Philadelphia."

"What if I said I found something right in Punxsutawney?"

"You have a job? Here?"

"Not yet, but I have an interview. I stopped off at the Weather Discovery Center to check it out. They had a scout troop going through the whole museum, playing with all the displays. Rain. Lightning, even making little tornadoes. All the things I loved about weather when I was a kid. The director mistook me for a parent, and we got to talking. They've been wanting to add a meteorologist to the staff to set up programs for older visitors, high school classes, maybe oversee college interns."

"And you'd like that?"

"Frankly, the job wouldn't be the only thing keeping me here." He put his arm around her shoulder. "But it sounds more rewarding than running charts for the clean energy industries. It's not a sure thing at this point, but we hit it off, and she seemed enthusiastic about my chances."

"She?"

"Afraid of a little competition?"

"Should I be?"

"Maybe. For sixty, she was rather well preserved."

Amy laughed and met his gaze.

"If I were to stay," Guy said, "would you be willing to explore whatever this is going on between us?"

Amy turned in his arms to face him. "Test the weather, so to speak?" She leaned her head on his shoulder. "I think I would."

"You know," said Guy, "I expressed my doubts about the ability of groundhogs to predict the weather, but if you wanted to, we still have plenty of time to head over to Gobbler's Knob and watch Phil look for his shadow."

She lifted her face, that playful little smile that he adored tickling the corner of her mouth. "Who's Phil?"

And he kissed her.

Dear Reader,

As with every story we write, the lessons woven throughout are lessons God is teaching us more than something we hope to teach. It's difficult to write a story set in a community called Panic without being drawn to a theme of dealing with fear. Circumstances abound—pandemics and other illnesses, financial crises, political strife and instabilities both at home and abroad—all of which can certainly raise our stress levels. Often our first impulse can be to run away or to muddle through and try to deal with these issues on our own.

*A Heart Divided* deals with fear—the crippling kind that verges on panic. For these characters, the fear is war and the prejudices that are often born from it. While that concept may seem distant to us today, the battles we face, while not so overwhelming as war, can be just as fearsome if not dealt with the way God intended—with His Word and the Sword of the Spirit in hand.

In *No Fear in Love,* we dropped a character into a strange place where he knew nobody and then stripped away his ability to deal with those issues on his own. It's often in the place where we discover ourselves insufficient that we learn what faith and trust are all about. In that place, we discover how good God really is.

It's no coincidence that Panic, Pennsylvania, is where these stories are set. Our heavenly Father always knows what we have need of, and in this instance, both Guy and Amy learn to trust Him through every doubt and fear.

That's why we're so very grateful that we get to do what we love…writing stories that hopefully inspire others to spend time thinking on those good and perfect things of God. We pray that this story blesses you, dear reader, and that you find comfort and hope in these pages just as we did.

Sincerely,<br>
Elizabeth Ludwig and Barbara Early

# About the Authors

### Elizabeth Ludwig

Elizabeth Ludwig is a *USA Today* bestselling author and speaker, often attending conferences where she lectures on editing for fiction writers, crafting effective novel proposals, and conducting successful editor/agent interviews. Elizabeth was honored to be awarded a HOLT Medallion for her book, *A Tempting Taste of Mystery*, part of the Sugarcreek Amish Mysteries series from Guideposts. Most recently, she was named a dual-finalist in the 2020 Selah Awards for *Garage Sale Secret*, part of the Mysteries of Lancaster County series from Guideposts.

### Barbara Early

Barbara Early earned an engineering degree, but after years of doing nothing but math, she developed a sudden allergy to the subject and decided to choose another occupation. Before she settled on a life of fictional crime, she was a schoolteacher, a pastor's wife, and an amateur puppeteer. She and her husband live in the snowy (but delightful) Buffalo, New York, suburbs, where she enjoys crafts, watching classic movies and campy television, playing board games, and spending time with her two granddaughters.

# Story Behind the Name

*Panic, Pennsylvania*

Panic, Pennsylvania, is a small, rural community in Jefferson County, roughly nine miles from Punxsutawney, where, every February 2, the nation pins its hopes of an early spring on whether or not a certain groundhog sees its shadow. This tradition sprang from the Amish community, and today Panic still consists mainly of farms of both the "English" and Amish varieties.

The community remained unnamed until the late 1800s when their application for a post office required one. Several stories account for their choice of "Panic." Most sources suggest the name likely derives its origin from the Panic of 1873, a financial crisis also called the Great Depression until it was usurped by an even greater one.

Others propose the name sprang from an encounter between a bear and an axe-wielding pioneer—although which of them was the most panicked remains unclear.

A third theory proposes that the community chose a different name altogether, but another town beat them to it. They had to pick a new one quickly or forgo their post office, and under the pressure, they *panicked*.

Panic is found on (some) maps adjacent to the communities of Desire, Paradise, and, of course, Punxsutawney, derived from the Lenape for "Land of the Sandflies."

# Winnie's Busy Day Vegetable Soup

**Ingredients:**

2 cups of your favorite broth (or bouillon cubes with water added)

1 28-ounce can petite diced tomatoes (or crushed tomatoes)

1 small jar pureed carrots (yes, baby food!)

1 16-ounce bag frozen mixed vegetables

1/3 cup pearl barley, uncooked

1 tablespoon Italian seasoning

1 tablespoon sugar

1/2 teaspoon celery salt

1/2 teaspoon salt (or more or less to taste)

1/2 teaspoon black pepper (or more or less to taste)

**Directions:**

Put all ingredients into a pot and simmer on medium heat, stirring occasionally, until vegetables and barley are tender, 30 to 40 minutes.

*Variation: Replace tomatoes with 1 14.5-ounce can diced tomatoes plus 1 15-ounce can sweet potato puree. Increase broth to 3 cups.*

*Read on for a sneak peek of another exciting book in the Love's a Mystery series!*

# Love's a Mystery in
# Embarrass, Wisconsin
## by Becky Melby & Cynthia Ruchti

**At First Blush**

By Becky Melby

*Embarrass, Wisconsin*
*December 1, 1901*

Lilly Galloway set perfectly plated pieces of coffee-chocolate chess pie in front of three of the Galloway Hotel Sunday regulars then held her breath, waiting for a nod or scowl from the shortest man. Chef Jean-Claude Pascal chewed and swallowed then poked at the sugared crust with his fork. Finally, when Lilly thought her lungs might burst, a smile tipped one side of his moustache. *"Magnifique,* as always."

Lilly inhaled then turned to the tall, skinny member of the trio. "How are things at the camp, Jimmie? Everything on schedule for the season?"

Jimmie fiddled with the red bandana knotted below his Adam's apple. "Not if you ask Lamoreaux."

She willed away the blush the name triggered. "He's always a bit anxious right before logging starts."

"Yep. More so this year on account of our numbers are down. But don't you worry, me and Axe ain't goin' nowhere. Your pies and this little Frenchman's grub will keep the both of us here until some dandy sweeps you off your feet and carries you back to the city."

A picture flashed in her mind of a clean-shaven man with slicked hair and an ascot tie throwing her over his shoulder and carting her back to Milwaukee. She wanted neither the dandy nor the city. She laughed and turned to the older, thickset man known as Axe. "How many years have you been a sawyer?"

"Far too many. Time to look for a job that pays more and doesn't threaten to kill me every time I turn my back." He tapped the folded newspaper at his right elbow. "Might just take up kidnapping. It's been almost a year since that boy went missing in Omaha. The kidnapper got twenty-five grand, returned the kid, and never got caught."

Lilly shook her head. "I'll bake you a special loaf of bread when I come visit you in prison."

Axe's laugh rumbled across the table. "Knew I could count on you."

"Kidnappin's too complicated. Train robbin's the way to go." Jimmie's scraggly mustache wobbled as he grinned. "Those guys who got the money box last month are still dodgin' the law."

Lilly rolled her eyes. "You two enjoy planning your next big crime, but some of us need to make an honest living, so I will bid you adieu."

While she didn't mind waiting on tables, the kitchen was the place where she felt she was doing what God had gifted her to do. After washing her hands, she finished fluting the crust on the seventh pie she'd made that morning and began the part she enjoyed the most.

Scooping up the scraps of dough she'd trimmed, she squished them into a ball then rolled it out flat. In a gesture she could do in her sleep now, she swished the tip of a paring knife in four arcs, making two half circles on each side, then added two antennae sprouting from the top. With practiced care, she lifted the butterfly cutout and placed it in the center of the lumpy pie bulging with apple slices.

"There's no time for that frivolous frippery today." The comment came on an irritated sigh. Bette, Lilly's half sister, leaned on the doorframe, nodding her head toward the dining room. Still wearing her church dress, she looked far too stylish to be waiting on tables. Bette raised an arm and dabbed her forehead with her sleeve. "Sunday crowd's bigger than usual, and the loggers are in rare form. Better make more chocolate and another cherry while you're at it, or you'll not have enough to send back with Jean-Claude. And have you thought ahead to order enough baking supplies for Christmas? We could get snow any day and the train might not..."

As Bette rambled on, Lilly heard a soft *tsk* behind her. Dottie, their cook, the little round woman who woke before the sun every morning to fry rashers of bacon and dozens of eggs while prepping sides of beef and whole chickens for the dinner and supper crowds, never tried too hard to hide her dislike of the way Bette treated Lilly. Her quick wit had saved Lilly's outlook on more days than she could possibly count.

Repressing a smile triggered by that one little syllable uttered by Dottie, Lilly cut six slits fanning out from her "frivolous frippery." She sprinkled the top with sugar and slid the pie onto the middle rack of the cookstove. After closing the oven door and checking the fire, she bent down, reached into a barrel, and filled her apron with green apples, enough for two Dutch apple pies. Listening to Dottie sing "Rock of Ages" while mapping out her next few steps—*make enough dough for eight crusts, drain the cherries, brew coffee, mix the cocoa and sugar*—kept her thoughts from falling into Bette's Slough of Despond.

If Bette had her way, she'd turn the Closed sign over for the last time and hop a train back to Milwaukee in a heartbeat. Lilly didn't share her sister's longing to return to "decorum and civility." She'd been sixteen in 1895 when her parents died of smallpox and Bette had insisted she come north to live with her, practically a stranger though they shared the same blood. Some of it, anyway.

She and Bette had the same father, but different mothers. Bette's mother had died when she was twelve. Two years later, her father had remarried, and a year after that, Lilly was born. She and Bette had only lived under the same roof for four years before Bette moved to the tiny village of Embarrass to start a hotel with her intended. Sadly, the man Bette was promised to had been killed in a logging accident two weeks before their wedding and only days before he was to quit logging for the safe role of a hotelier. As if grief were not enough of a burden to bear, Thomas had left the hotel to Bette. Along with its mortgage.

Bette was stuck—in a town whose name meant the same thing. Though travelers assumed something scandalous or humorous had occurred in the little river town, the French word *Embarrasser*, not only meant "to embarrass." It also meant "to obstruct." The river on which the village sat was often choked with logs during the spring season, causing the French-Canadian lumberjacks to coin the name *Revieve Embarrasser*. English settlers had modified the name, and the town and the river had been known as Embarrass ever since.

While Lilly did have some fond memories of school friends, attending teas with her mother, and downtown shopping trips, she'd always been a nature lover, preferring to spend time in the small woods behind their modest Milwaukee home. Here, in the expansive Northwoods, she could ignore her sister's reprimands about what constituted "appropriate behavior" for a young woman. Here, no one batted an eye when she donned breeches to ride horseback or wandered in the forest with a butterfly net.

Recently, she had tried to take Bette's instructions a bit more seriously...for one reason alone. A tall, broad-shouldered, witty, sky-blue-eyed reason. Not that it did any good. No matter what she wore, how she fixed her hair, how she smiled, fawned, or fluttered her eyelashes, Élan Lamoreaux still saw her as the gangly sixteen-year-old city girl she'd been when they first met. The foreman of the *Soleil Rouge* lumber camp was as dense as the century-old white pines he felled.

And...he was here. Now.

Peering through the half-open kitchen door, Lilly stared down the long hallway at the man who stood in the foyer blocking the light from the window in the front door. Like the giant woodsman in the French-Canadian lumbermen's tall tales, the one whose footsteps created the thousands of lakes in Wisconsin and Minnesota, he was larger than life and stronger than any other two men put together. At least in her mind, he was.

He took a few steps, his gaze sweeping the dining room. She held her breath, wondering if he sought her. And then he waved. Her heart thudded against her ribs. Clutching her apron with her left hand, she raised her right hand in a shaky greeting…as Élan joined Axe, Jimmie, and Jean-Claude, whose hands were raised just like hers. Mortified, and hoping he hadn't seen her wave, she dropped her hand. At the last second, before picking up his menu, he looked her way. And winked.

A dozen green apples tumbled onto the plank floor, rolling under the stove and the table. And out the partially open door into the dining room.

Lilly sank to her knees as a single, determined apple kept rolling. And rolling. Stopping under a table. An inch from Élan's boots.

Jimmie and Axe guffawed.

Her face burned. Her pulse slammed against her eardrums the way she wanted to bang her head against the wall. Head down, she concentrated on picking up apples, counting them under her breath, as if her focused attention would make it look like she hadn't noticed the wayward fruit. Maybe he hadn't either. Maybe—

"I believe you dropped this, *Papillon*."

That name. The one only he called her. French for butterfly. It had the same effect as his wink, discombobulating her senses.

"Thanks, M-moose." Using the English translation of his name, the nickname she'd given him years ago, made her appear casual, unflustered. Didn't it? As if it was an everyday occurrence to be kneeling in her kitchen at the feet of the most handsome man in all of Wisconsin. A man who had just winked at her.

Slowly, she lifted her blazing face, up and up, until she met those sky-blue eyes. Eyes that danced with mirth.

She couldn't let him see her turning into a puddle of warm molasses at his feet. With a bracing breath for courage, she stood. Too fast. The kitchen tilted. A large hand grabbed her upper arm, steadying her.

"Are you all right?"

*No. No, no, no.* Not even close to being all right. But she wasn't about to let him see her swooning like a schoolgirl. "Just stood up too fast." She tried to snatch the apple from the hand that wasn't still gripping her arm, but he wouldn't let go. "I'm f-fine." Her lips didn't seem to want to do what her brain told them to.

"Maybe you need to eat something." Grinning, he lifted the apple to her lips.

Behind him, Bette cleared her throat, and Élan lowered the apple and flattened against the doorframe.

"Excuse me, Mr. Lamoreaux." Bette pushed past him with a glare that threatened to bring on winter a month early. "I have the same rules in my kitchen as you have in your camp. No unauthorized persons in the work area." Turning, she simply said, "Lilly." The one-word warning conveyed paragraphs. Paragraphs she'd likely hear over supper. *When the dining room is open, we do nothing but work. We do not fraternize with the customers, especially the loggers. You must do nothing to convey the wrong impression.*

Lilly grabbed the apple. This time he let go of it. With a nod and another wink, Moose turned and walked away.

He'd *winked*. Twice. She couldn't remember him ever doing that before. What did it mean? People winked at children who did something childishly entertaining. Was that it? Was he simply laughing at her clumsiness? Men winked at women for many reasons, many of them wrong reasons. But Élan, for all his burly roughness, was a gentleman.

So what did it mean? As she peeled more apples, mixed enough topping for three Dutch apple pies, and drained two quarts of cherries in cheesecloth, her overactive mind pondered the winks. Lost in thought, she was stirring ingredients for two coffee-chocolate chess pies, a recipe she'd created herself, when another shadow blocked the light in the kitchen doorway. Well, some of the light.

Lilly grinned as Chef Jean-Claude Pascal, all five-foot-four of him, stepped into the kitchen. At her insistence, and over Bette's protests, Jean-Claude had been deemed an "authorized" person. This little man, old enough to be her father, had been her first friend when she moved to this tiny wilderness town. Their friendship had started the day she served her first pie to hotel guests. He'd come storming into the kitchen, shouting in French, "*Madame, on mange d'abord avec les yeux.*" It meant "Madam, we eat with our eyes first!" Though humiliated when he'd stuck the hastily dished plate of blueberry pie under her nose, it was a phrase she had come to adore. *Présentation*, as Jean-Claude so often exclaimed, was everything. It was he who had encouraged her to create her own "signature in pie crust"—her butterfly cutouts.

Jean-Claude greeted her as he always did, with a kiss on the cheek. "How are things in the kitchen of ze famous Lilly Galloway?" He reached for a clean silver spoon, dipped it in the crumbly flour, sugar, and butter Dutch apple topping, and tasted, pulling the spoon slowly from his lips.

Once again, Lilly wondered if she'd be rewarded with a smile or an opportunity to learn something new.

"*Délicieux.*" Jean-Claude pressed his thumb and forefinger together and kissed them with a loud smack. "Someone has taught you well."

He set the spoon on the table and watched as she stirred the ingredients for the chess pie just the way he'd taught her, with "vigor but not haste."

"It has been a busy morning. I have seven pies for you."

"*Merci.* That will keep the ravenous wolves and their guests at bay tonight." Though Jean-Claude rarely had a kind word for the men to whom he served three meals a day, Lilly knew most of it was in jest.

"Need I tell you what you often tell me, that your talents are wasted here?"

He waved away her compliment. "*Vous aussi?* Another voice to tickle my ears and tempt me to do something dangerous. If I open my own restaurant, it will become a success, of course, and that can only mean trouble."

"But that was so long ago. Surely no one remembers a handful of gems disappearing eleven years ago. The rich woman probably found her missing jewels soon after you left London. Isn't it likely everyone now knows you didn't take them, and you would be welcomed back to the Savoy with open arms? Not that I want you to leave this country. What about Chicago, or New York?"

"Alas, I could never leave my Mamie."

All she knew about Jean-Claude's lady friend was that she lived in another town and he visited her every Sunday. She was the reason he had come to Wisconsin. "Take her with you!"

A wistful look crossed his face. "Sadly, that would never happen."

"Well, I give up then, but a classically trained chef hiding out in the Northwoods is…" She fumbled for the right word. "It's blasphemy!"

Eyes wide, Jean-Claude stared at her. "How did you arrive at that?"

"God has gifted you with skills. No one, maybe no one in all of North America, can make chocolate mousse, *tarte flambée, hachis Parmentier,* or *soupe de poisson* like you." The French names rolled off her tongue, so much more elegant than flaming tart, meat pie, and fish stew. "And you are fixing these delicacies—these heavenly creations that bless one's palate with flavors found nowhere else—for a bunch of loud, brash, heathen louts. It is akin to casting pearls before swine!"

Jean-Claude held one hand to his forehead. "Oh, my dear, you have convicted me. You have pierced my heart with your effusive compliments." The slightest of smiles teased one corner of his handlebar moustache. "How can I possibly return to my old cookstove and sad little camp kitchen when greatness awaits?" He thrust out his arm…and came within inches of slapping Bette in the face.

Bette huffed and took a step back. "*Mis*ter Pascal, kindly stop bothering the help."

As she whipped past him, Jean-Claude stuck out his tongue then smiled knowingly at Lilly. "Maybe," he whispered, "when I escape to New York City, I will take the famous butterfly pie girl with me. But, alas, I believe that would break the heart of a certain someone. Someone the size of a bull moose who could easily break me."

For the third time in minutes, a man winked at her. At least this one she could decipher.

# A Note from the Editors

We hope you enjoyed another book in the Love's a Mystery series, published by Guideposts. For over seventy-five years Guideposts, a nonprofit organization, has been driven by a vision of a world filled with hope. We aspire to be the voice of a trusted friend, a friend who makes you feel more hopeful and connected.

By making a purchase from Guideposts, you join our community in touching millions of lives, inspiring them to believe that all things are possible through faith, hope, and prayer. Your continued support allows us to provide uplifting resources to those in need. Whether through our online communities, websites, apps, or publications, we strive to inspire our audiences, bring them together, comfort, uplift, entertain, and guide them.

To learn more, please go to guideposts.org.

**While you are waiting for the next fascinating story in the *Love's a Mystery* series, check out some other Guideposts mystery series!**

# Savannah Secrets

Welcome to Savannah, Georgia, a picture-perfect Southern city known for its manicured parks, moss-covered oaks, and antebellum architecture. Walk down one of the cobblestone streets, and you'll come upon Magnolia Investigations. It is here where two friends have joined forces to unravel some of Savannah's deepest secrets. Tag along as clues are exposed, red herrings discarded, and thrilling surprises revealed. Find inspiration in the special bond between Meredith Bellefontaine and Julia Foley. Cheer the friends on as they listen to their hearts and rely on their faith to solve each new case that comes their way.

*The Hidden Gate*
*The Fallen Petal*
*Double Trouble*
*Whispering Bells*
*Where Time Stood Still*

## LOVE'S A MYSTERY

*The Weight of Years*
*Willful Transgressions*
*Season's Meetings*
*Southern Fried Secrets*
*The Greatest of These*
*Patterns of Deception*
*The Waving Girl*
*Beneath a Dragon Moon*
*Garden Variety Crimes*
*Meant for Good*
*A Bone to Pick*
*Honeybees & Legacies*
*True Grits*
*Sapphire Secret*
*Jingle Bell Heist*
*Buried Secrets*
*A Puzzle of Pearls*
*Facing the Facts*
*Resurrecting Trouble*
*Forever and a Day*

# MYSTERIES OF MARTHA'S VINEYARD

Priscilla Latham Grant has inherited a lighthouse! So with not much more than a strong will and a sore heart, the recent widow says goodbye to her lifelong Kansas home and heads to the quaint and historic island of Martha's Vineyard, Massachusetts. There, she comes face-to-face with adventures, which include her trusty canine friend, Jake, three delightful cousins she didn't know she had, and Gerald O'Bannon, a handsome Coast Guard captain—plus head-scratching mysteries that crop up with surprising regularity.

*A Light in the Darkness*
*Like a Fish Out of Water*
*Adrift*
*Maiden of the Mist*
*Making Waves*
*Don't Rock the Boat*
*A Port in the Storm*
*Thicker Than Water*
*Swept Away*
*Bridge Over Troubled Waters*

## LOVE'S A MYSTERY

*Smoke on the Water*
*Shifting Sands*
*Shark Bait*
*Seascape in Shadows*
*Storm Tide*
*Water Flows Uphill*
*Catch of the Day*
*Beyond the Sea*
*Wider Than an Ocean*
*Sheeps Passing in the Night*
*Sail Away Home*
*Waves of Doubt*
*Lifeline*
*Flotsam & Jetsam*
*Just Over the Horizon*

# MIRACLES & MYSTERIES OF MERCY HOSPITAL

Four talented women from very different walks of life witness the miracles happening around them at Mercy Hospital and soon become fast friends. Join Joy Atkins, Evelyn Perry, Anne Mabry, and Shirley Bashore as, together, they solve the puzzling mysteries that arise at this Charleston, South Carolina, historic hospital—rumored to be under the protection of a guardian angel. Come along as our quartet of faithful friends solve mysteries, stumble upon a few of the hospital's hidden and forgotten passageways, and discover historical treasures along the way! This fast-paced series is filled with inspiration, adventure, mystery, delightful humor, and loads of Southern charm!

*Where Mercy Begins*
*Prescription for Mystery*
*Angels Watching Over Me*
*A Change of Art*
*Conscious Decisions*
*Surrounded by Mercy*
*Broken Bonds*

## LOVE'S A MYSTERY

*Mercy's Healing*
*To Heal a Heart*
*A Cross to Bear*
*Merciful Secrecy*
*Sunken Hopes*
*Hair Today, Gone Tomorrow*
*Pain Relief*
*Redeemed by Mercy*
*A Genius Solution*
*A Hard Pill to Swallow*
*Ill at Ease*
*'Twas the Clue Before Christmas*

# Find more inspiring stories in these best-loved Guideposts fiction series!

## Mysteries of Lancaster County
Follow the Classen sisters as they unravel clues and uncover hidden secrets in Mysteries of Lancaster County. As you get to know these women and their friends, you'll see how God brings each of them together for a fresh start in life.

## Secrets of Wayfarers Inn
Retired schoolteachers find themselves owners of an old warehouse-turned-inn that is filled with hidden passages, buried secrets, and stunning surprises that will set them on a course to puzzling mysteries from the Underground Railroad.

## Tearoom Mysteries Series
Mix one stately Victorian home, a charming lakeside town in Maine, and two adventurous cousins with a passion for tea and hospitality. Add a large scoop of intriguing mystery, and sprinkle generously with faith, family, and friends, and you have the recipe for *Tearoom Mysteries*.

## Ordinary Women of the Bible
Richly imagined stories—based on facts from the Bible—have all the plot twists and suspense of a great mystery, while bringing you fascinating insights on what it was like to be a woman living in the ancient world.

**To learn more about these books, visit Guideposts.org/Shop**